How to tell your

FORTUNE

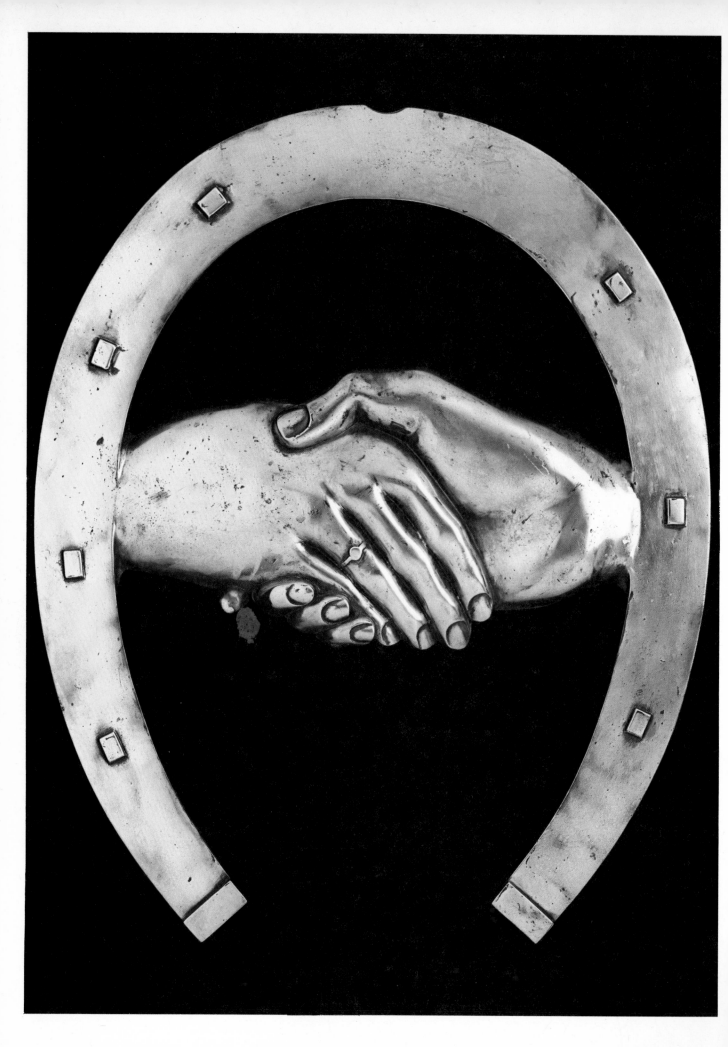

How to tell your
FORTUNE

Peter Brent

Credits
Frontispiece Don McAllester.
Chris Barker pp. 15, 25, 49, 50, 51
52-53, 55, 64. Steve Bicknell p. 34.
The Bodleian Library, Oxford pp. 9.
32, 33. The British Museum, London
pp. 32, 64. Alan Duns pp. 22-23.
Mary Evans Picture Library pp. 7, 29,
62. Malcolm Scoular pp. 26, 37, 45,
60, 63. Snark International p. 8.
Michael JamesWard p. 14.
Illustrations by Maggie Raynor.
Artwork makeup by Roy Flooks.

Distributed in the USA by Amiel Book Distributors Inc,
31 West 46th Street, New York 10036

Published by Marshall Cavendish Publications Limited,
58 Old Compton Street, London W1V 5PA

This volume first published 1975

Printed in Great Britain
by Ben Johnson and Company Ltd, York

LOC No. 08148-0643-0

Introduction

Cards, hands, tea-leaves, dice and dominoes—even the bumps on your head—any of these can be used to read your fortune. Whether you take it seriously or just think of it as an amusing pastime, you will be able to use all the various methods to entertain your friends with your new-found talent. There are details of the background and techniques needed for the different ways of telling fortunes and revealing character. Some of the information has an 'old world' sound: this is mainly because there was a great interest in many aspects of fortune telling in Victorian times and much of the information comes from nineteenth century sources.

Here you can find out about frivolous superstitions, like the meaning of moles or itches on various parts of the body, and more serious methods too, like palmistry and I Ching. The sample palm analyses included were made by experts who know nothing at all about their clients and yet were astonishingly accurate.

Much of fortune telling depends on interpretation of the 'signs' in the cards or at the bottom of the cup, so to help you develop your skills to the full there are many examples to show you how to weave seemingly unconnected meanings and symbols into fascinating readings.

Contents

What is fortune telling?

Fortune telling falls into two parts: the divining of the future and the reading of character and how it has been shaped by events in the past. Palmistry alone combines both of these facets — the other methods in this book are concerned solely with one or the other. This book can be used in several different ways — for serious attempts to read character or the future; for fun and entertainment among friends, or simply for the curiosity value of a collection of past beliefs. There are sections which fall into each of these categories. Numerology uses the logic of mathematics to bring order out of apparent chaos. Palm reading and phrenology — the reading of lumps on the head — can be amusing to try out on friends and the collection of past beliefs — the meanings of moles, for

example — and the section on tea-leaf reading, make fascinating reading.

Methods

Since time immemorial man has tried to give Fate an opportunity to make its intentions known by using the operations of Chance. And it is from these that all methods of foretelling the future developed. Some are no longer seriously used; some, however, many people take very seriously. I Ching, one of the oldest methods, has many devoted adherents, and the Tarot pack continues to draw believers. Perhaps it is the more obscure and complicated methods which inspire faith. The pack of cards used in everyday life to play poker, patience or snap has no longer the same aura. We find it difficult to

believe it can reveal our future. But the Tarot — its signs and figures clearly fixed in the remote past — we feel can tell us something. It is as though Fate, being mysterious, needs a mysterious vessel to work through.

In the following pages there are fortune telling methods both old and new. All of them are interesting and fun to use even if you do not place much faith in some of them.

Character

If you can tell fortunes or reveal character you will find that people gather around like bees after honey, clamouring to be told about themselves and their character. And this is one sure way to get conversation going at a party! A further dimension

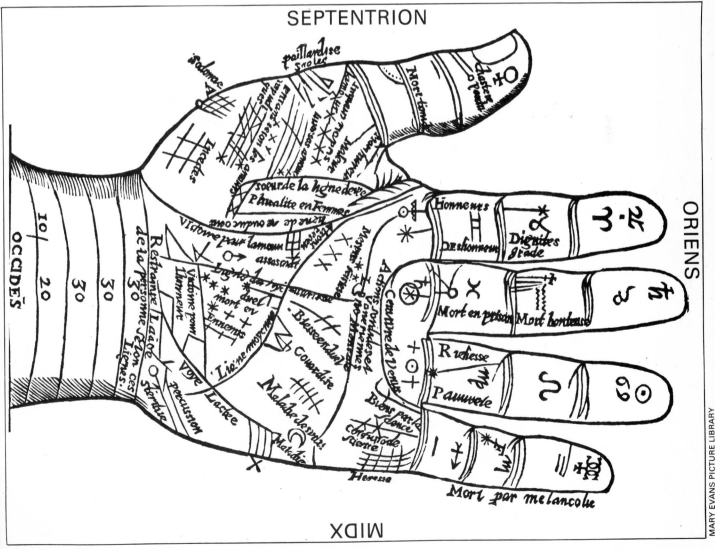

is added to your self-knowledge when your character is told. If the fortune teller is on target there is the surprise of having your views of yourself reinforced or modified or your self-deceptions shattered.

The fascination lies in the fact that things you thought were only known to you are suddenly revealed as apparent to others too. And this is revealed objectively. It is not simply other people's views of your character which happen to coincide with your own. The fortune teller has divined them from an outside source, whether cards, a palm print or the lumps on your head. And even the sceptic can be somewhat unnerved by accuracy obtained like this without rational provision of data.

Yet this is not so strange; finger prints are accepted as unique (they are used regularly in the detection of criminals), so why should not the same apply to palm prints? It could be that what is unique to you might in some way reveal something of your inner self.

The future

The future is fascinating to everyone. You frequently consider the past and remember how often you have been overtaken by surprise, how many opportunities you missed because they presented themselves too suddenly, how may offers of help you spurned because you misunderstood them. 'If only I'd known', you murmur.

As a result even the most sceptical people keep some corner of the mind free for an unacknowledged hope that perhaps, in some way, such knowledge just might be obtainable. There the mind allows itself to accept omens, superstitions, portents and the telling of fortunes. And even if you don't actually believe implicitly in these it is possible that alternative courses of action may be indicated which had not previously occurred to you. You might even consider acting upon them.

On the other hand, if you believe in an underlying pattern in events, that the seeds of the future lie in the present, then you believe in Fate.

Some methods of telling character can be claimed to be scientific because they relate directly to the subject rather than the operations of chance working through cards, say, or tea leaves.

Phrenology, on the other hand, started with scientific pretensions and has now largely fallen into disrepute. But it remains amusing, and a good party

game guaranteed to claim the attention of the person whose lumps you are reading.

Telling your own fortune

You can attempt to peer into your own future by using cards or the I Ching. In general, however, fortune telling demands a 'diviner' and a 'client'. This is because you cannot stand far enough away from yourself to interpret your own future without bending the facts slightly to suit your wishes.

Learning by heart?

It is, of course, better if you can memorize the meanings of the cards — both ordinary and Tarot — tea-leaf formations and so forth. If you do then there will be no hesitations in your readings, no searching through this book for the relevant passage!

On the other hand, you can simply familiarize yourself with the meanings and then refer to the text as necessary. This can be an even more impressive method. Friends and acquaintances might mistrust your reading if they think you are using your imagination rather freely. But they will probably tend to believe and accept your predictions if they see you referring to a text and then interpreting it. Interpretation is, perhaps, the most important factor in fortune telling so the need to refer back to the book does not detract too much from your impact or your claim to be a fortune teller.

Be responsible

Beware when reading other people's futures. Many people, however much they protest disbelief, will half believe or be disturbed by any prognostications of doom and disaster that you may give. Use your tact and discretion in deciding how much to reveal, and when. If reading futures or characters in public — at a party, say — be careful. Your client may be secretly pleased to hear he will change his life, go abroad or marry three times — but his wife may not be.

Intuition and imagination

When you reveal the character or tell the fortunes of others your intuition, sympathy and awareness all come into play. Fortune telling when done face to face depends largely on the interaction of minds. Mutual sympathy is important. If you the fortune teller

are responsive to and aware of the client's reactions, the reading has a better chance of success. Let your subconscious and imagination have full rein. Many of us are more intuitive than we think and if you temporarily discard logical thought processes you may be surprised at your own powers of discernment.

At the simplest level fortune telling can be an amusing party trick and a very good way of getting to know people. It can also offer clues to greater self-knowledge and a chance to glimpse future possibilities.

The language of signs

Long before writing was invented, man used a rich vocabulary of signs to express hopes and fears about his own life and the world that surrounded him.

The five pointed star is one of the most ancient signs — certainly older than writing. It was believed to be a protection against witches.

Three arrows bound together — a sign of unity.

A sign used to cast out evil spirits.

Omens, oracles and signs

There is hardly anything which moves which has not at one time served as an omen, hardly any human activity which was not surrounded with its own superstitions. The direction a bed faced has been thought significant — for riches, the head should be to the East, for a long life, to the South. Money was supposed to come to you if you sneezed to the right, good news if you dropped and smashed an egg or had a shoelace which kept coming undone.

Fortune might attend you if you picked up a pin, met the same person twice on the same journey or broke uncoloured glass (but if that glass was a mirror or a bottle then bad luck would follow). The sight of bellows and the burning of bones was once considered unlucky. If you wanted to avoid evil fortune you had, apparently, to not cut your hair before the new moon, avoid meeting grave-diggers, be careful never to cross two forks or two knives, and not mend clothes while you were wearing them. You should also never — unless you wanted to tempt fate — put your left shoe on before your right, break a pair of scissors, sit on a table without keeping one foot on the ground and, of course, never open an umbrella indoors.

It is as though everyone felt they were on the verge of disaster all the time, kept from ill-fortune only by a series of inconsequential yet desperately important actions. At any moment one might unknowingly trigger off disaster. The spilling of salt, the breaking of a plate, even a sneeze — especially, it seems, on a Monday or Friday — could summon bad luck which had been lying in wait. If one believed all this then every action, every occurrence became an oracular pronouncement. All that was necessary was to know the appropriate meaning and one was then forewarned and prepared for what the future held in store.

Omens

People believed that Fate was constantly active and, therefore, that every-thing which occurred had a fateful message to convey. Every passing cloud, bird or breeze, every accident of nature, became part of the code by which one's future fate could be revealed so men scanned the earth and sky for omens.

Even now sometimes you probably catch yourself out not walking under a ladder, feeling slightly worried about breaking a mirror or waiting for the second magpie to appear. It is not necessarily that you believe in such omens, just that having heard them from childhood there is a vague feeling that perhaps you might, after all, be tempting fate. And people who do disregard them — walking deliberately under every ladder they see — often do so with a certain air of defiance!

However, whether or not you choose to believe in them, certain events and phenomena have, over the centuries, been given particular meanings. Some of the better-known ones are given below.

Animals

Carrying their unconscious forecasts of a good or a disastrous future, these too were thought to be the innocent messengers of Fate.

Bat Bad luck, especially if it cries while flying.

Cat There is doubt about the significance of this mysterious beast. Black, it may be good or bad; experience would have to tell. But to kill one is thought to be disastrous, and if one unaccountably leaves your house, it could mean catastrophe.

Dog Much less involved with fortune telling, but an omen of death if it howls at the moon, although it offers no precise warning of where death intends to strike.

Goat Good luck.

Hare Unfortunate, especially if one crosses your path.

These charming animal drawings are taken from a medieval manuscript. Even today country dwellers still think of animals as harbingers of fate.

Hedgehog Good fortune, especially if met going in the opposite direction.

Horse Piebald, a good omen. (If seen tail first, however, a friend may meet misfortune.) A white horse seen by lovers will bring them good luck.

Mouse White or brown, it means happiness, especially in love; grey, danger threatens.

Pig A bad omen, especially if met immediately after marriage.

Rat Good, if white; bad, if black.

Sheep In a flock, good fortune, especially if approaching.

Squirrel Happiness will be found soon after seeing one.

Birds

Because the flight of birds is so unpredictable, yet so apparently purposeful, their appearance has often been taken as a portent of good or evil fortune.

Crow A bad omen, especially if seen to the left.

Cuckoo Not seen, but heard, it foretells prosperity, especially if it is heard to the right.

Dove A happy omen, particularly for those about to marry.

Gull Settling on a ship, a happy sign for those about to sail in her. But to be touched by a gull in flight is said to foretell the death of someone close.

Hawk Be watchful — powerful enemies threaten. (This is supposed to be especially true if the bird is seen to the left.)

Kingfisher A scandal threatens.

Magpie One, especially on the left, is an omen of death. Two, however, are very lucky and signify that good fortune will follow within three days.

Owl Always bad luck. If it hoots three times, be especially careful.

Robin Good luck.

Sparrow Bad luck, except for lovers.

Swallow Very good fortune, especially early in Spring. If they build under your roof, good will follow. If you kill one, expect disaster.

Wagtail Fortunate, especially if approaching from the left.

Wren Good luck. (But at your peril either harm or frighten it.)

Insects

Their movements are difficult to forecast and their purposes obscure. Perhaps for this reason insects have always been taken to be messengers of Fate.

Ants A nest near your home is a good augury, but to be bitten by one means quarrels and strife.

Bee Good luck if it is trapped for a while in the house.

Cockroach If seen in an unusual place, it foretells a death.

Cricket Always and everywhere thought of as lucky. But if they suddenly abandon a house where they have been settled, disaster follows.

Grasshopper A journey, and good news.

Ladybird A good omen, especially if it has seven spots on its back.

Spider A doom-laden creature: seen in the morning, it means grief; at noon anxiety; in the evening, financial loss. A spider spinning a web means people are plotting. To kill one brings misfortune. However, if found on the body it is a harbinger of prosperity.

Wasp To be stung by a wasp indicates danger, probably through jealousy.

Patterns and shapes

As the patterns made by tea-leaves offer an irresistible temptation to look into the future so, too, did other apparently random formations. These were read in the same way as a tea-cup (see later for the meaning of the symbols). As with reading tea-leaves, it took some imagination and a great deal of concentration to understand the message offered by the symbols!

Egg whites
Take an egg, separate the white from the yolk, and pour the white into a bowl almost brimful of water. After 24 hours, clots will have formed which you should then be able to read.

Sealing wax
Heat a little sealing wax in a serving spoon or ladle. When it is melted, pour the wax into a bowl of clean water. The shapes that the wax forms will give you symbols which contain the answer you need.

Seeds
To discover the order in which certain events will occur, plant a seed for each event — but never enquire about more than five things. Put each seed in a separate pot. As far as possible give each pot the same amount of sunshine and water. The order in which the seedlings appear will give you the information you want. This process is likely to be somewhat lengthy so it is best not to enquire about events in the immediate future.

Simple questions

Several different methods were developed to answer questions which require only a simple affirmative or negative.

Burning paper
Write out a wish or a question on a slip of paper, place it face down on a plate and light it with a match. If all the paper is burnt, you will get what you want. But if only a part of it burns, though your wish may eventually be granted, this will not be for some time.

Cat's paw
If you have a cat, it too can give you a yes-or-no reply. Think of your question, then call your pet. If the right forepaw appears first around the door, the answer to your question is Yes.

Paper pieces
Write a different question on each of a number of pieces of paper (usually thirteen) and then place all the slips at the bottom of a bowl. Pour water into the bowl and wait for the first slip of paper to rise to the surface. The answer to the question on it will be Yes.

Paper squares
Cut two squares of paper, both the same size, and colour one black. Drop them both at the same time from an upstairs window. If the white one lands first, the answer is Yes.

Stones
Fill a wide bowl with water and murmur a question aloud as you drop a small stone into it. Count the ripples in the water — if the number is odd, the answer will be Yes.

Wedding ring
Tie a length of black thread around a gold wedding ring. Hold the other end of the thread in your left hand and then lower the ring into a glass of water. If it touches the right side of the glass then the answer to your question is Yes. If it touches the left, No. If it touches the side either nearest you or furthest away, you may take it that the oracle refuses to answer and should not be consulted for another 24 hours.

Itches

If one believes that all things have a meaning, then even a sudden irritation which demands to be scratched might be able to enlighten you in some way about your future. The message can be precisely deciphered by the place on the body where it has settled. Next time you have an itch, consider the

significance it might have.
Top of head Promotion.
Right cheek Someone is slandering you.
Left cheek Someone is complimenting you.
Right eye You will meet an old friend.
Left eye Disappointment awaits.
Inside nose Problems, grief.
Outside nose The saying is 'Kissed, cursed or meet with a fool', this to take place within the hour.
Lips Someone insults you behind your back.
Back of neck A relative will fall ill.
Right shoulder Legacy.
Left shoulder Sorrow.
Right elbow Goods news.
Left elbow Bad news.
Right palm Money comes your way.
Left palm Bills come your way.

Back Disappointment.
Stomach Invitation.
Loins Reconciliation.
Thighs A move.
Right knee Happy voyage.
Left knee Voyage beset with difficulty.
Shins An unpleasant surprise.
Ankles Marriage and/or a rise.
Sole (right foot) A journey with profit.
Sole (left foot) A journey which brings a loss.

Moles

Because one is born with these curious marks upon the body they were often thought significant. The essential information which they give depends

The position of significant moles on different parts of the body.

upon where the moles are placed. The bigger the mole, the more emphatically the attributes and fortunes it foretells will come into being. There are general points to watch for, too, because the shape of the mole has its importance. The rounder it is the more good fortune is implied. If the mole is raised, that means very good fortune indeed; an oval or pointed mole means bad luck, made even worse if its colour is dark, and worse again if it is hairy.

Forehead Right: intelligence, leading to fame and prosperity. Left: extravagance, fecklessness.
Eye Near the outer corner of either eye, placidity of temperament, frugality and thriftiness.
Eyebrow Right: happy and probably early marriage. Left: difficult marriage.
Ear Recklessness.
Cheek Right: happiness, especially in marriage. Left: difficulties, struggles.
Chin Success, prosperity, good fortune.
Mouth Happy, sensual disposition.
Jaw Bad health.
Nose Great fortune, travel, a developed sexuality.
Throat Rich marriage; ambitions attained.
Neck Many ups and downs, unexpected legacies, early set-backs but ultimate success.
Hand Natural ability, leading to success.
Arm Right: success. Left: financial anxiety.
Shoulder Hard and difficult times.
Breast Right: ups and downs of fortune. Left: in a man — fortune and happiness, in a woman — ardent temperament, sometimes leading to foolish attachments. Centre: adequate income, but no great wealth.
Abdomen A nature selfish and self-indulgent, lazy and perhaps greedy.
Back Frankness and generosity, but also arrogance and self-display. If very low: sensuality and self-indulgence.
Ribs Right: cowardice, indolence, insensitivity, boorishness. Left: the same, but less so and modified by humour.
Hips Strong, healthy children and numerous grandchildren.
Thigh Right: warmth of temperament, wealth, happiness in marriage. Left: loneliness, loss, poverty, although the temperament is equally warm.
Knee Right: ease in marriage and with finances. Left: rashness.
Ankle Refinement, leading in a man to dandyism. In a woman a sign of energy and hard work.
Foot Right: love of travelling. Left: swift intelligence.
Leg Right or left: laziness.

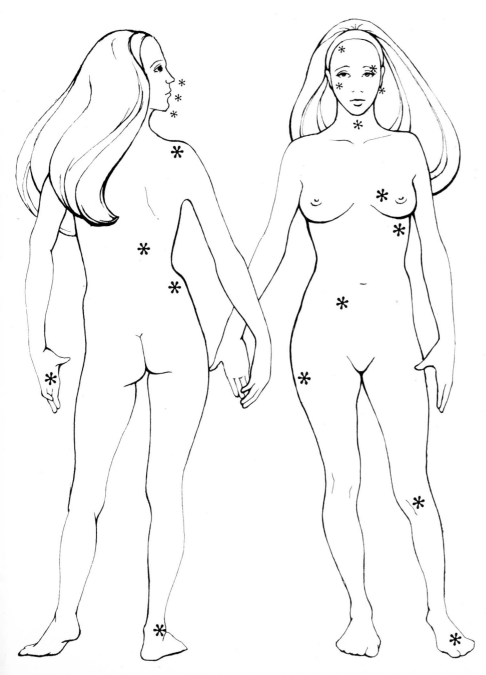

The trial of destiny

*Use this chart to tell your
own fortune as well as other people's.
The instructions are in the text.*

12 FORTUNE

Choose which subject you want to ask a question about — you can, if you like ask a question on each subject. Then take a pin, close your eyes and prick the pin into the section of your choice. The number the pin lands on gives the answer to your question. The inner point sections give a general indication of something about to happen to you — and here again you can choose a section. Close your eyes and proceed in the same way. If the pin fails to hit a number, fate is unwilling to answer your query.

Love
1. Many lovers.
2. One sincere lover, one false one.
3. A flirtation.
4. A senseless jest.
5. A lover who has not the courage to speak his mind.
6. You love and are not beloved again, — so banish the flame.

Courtship
1. The lover is sincere.
2. No wedlock is intended.
3. They are wavering in love.
4. A long courtship, to end in nothing.
5. It will end in marriage.
6. A sudden break.

Marriage
1. Happy, and of long duration.
2. Short, but prosperous and peaceful.
3. Not so soon as you expect, but happy in itself.
4. Not so happy in the end as the beginning promises.
5. A separation or divorce before death.
6. A paradise on earth awaits you in this respect.

Children
1. They will surround your table like olive-branches.
2. Several in number, — some as roses to you, and some will prove thorns.
3. One at most.
4. Not many.
5. One amongst your children will raise you to affluence, — they will all prove acceptable.
6. Illegitimate children will trouble you, yet perhaps not your own.

Kin
1. They will enrich you.
2. They will improverish you.
3. They will exalt you.
4. They will degrade you.
5. Some of your kindred will leave you

a valuable remembrance.
6. A death in the family.

Trade
1. You will never be indebted to it in your own person.
2. You will suddenly embark on it.
3. You will form a friendship with a trader.
4. You will lose by trade.
5. You will enter into partnership.
6. You will get rich by commerce.

Fortune
1. Changes every seven years will occur to you.
2. A steady life.
3. Sudden riches.
4. Fatal extravagance.
5. False promises will undo your peace.
6. A sudden fall and a great rise will mark your life.

Speculation
1. Success in the lottery.
2. Never speculate.
3. Chance luck.
4. Fortunate at cards.
5. You will be lucky at ventures in trade.
6. Luck in a wager to come.

The points
A a letter.
B a reproof.
C a loss.
D a gain.
E new appeal.
F a gift.
G a journey.
X a disappointment.
Y a feast.

1. A comfortable hour.
2. A change.
3. Bad news.
4. Good tidings.
5. A voyage.
6. A present of money.
7. A valentine.
8. A gift to wear.
9. A present for which you will pay dear.
10. You have lately practised some unworthy deception.
12. A period of anxiety.
13. Moment inauspicious. Try again.
15. You will soon lose something good by passion.
17. A long walk on a sudden occasion — try again. A cross betokens great joy — try once more.

Know that these points only refer to minor affairs, and such as will be speedily verified.

The reading of tea cups

The sediment in the cup one drinks from has in the past often been thought to provide clues to the drinker's fate, because it involves both the random and the personal.

Many people once thought that only those with 'psychic powers' could read cups. But no one has ever been able to define precisely what these powers are. You just may, whether consciously or not, possess them so do not let such a doctrine put you off. With knowledge and practice you may arrive at levels of perception which surprise you. This is by no means a precise science, however, and if you attempt it you will need to exercise your imagination and let your mind wander freely. Learning the meanings will not be enough.

Method

There are one or two basic points to remember. First, use a cup which can be easily read: one that is plain, and not straight-sided. Second, avoid a dusty tea. China tea is supposed to be the best, but any large-leaved mixture will do. (You can, of course, follow exactly the same procedure to read coffee grounds.) To provide the necessary personal link it is also thought to be vital that the subject actually drinks the cup of tea or coffee. In order to obtain the pictures you need, let your client drink almost the whole cup and then swill the remaining teaspoonful around a few times. (Some people insist on a ritual element in this

swirling of the dregs, and say it must be done only with the left hand and either three or seven times.)

Next turn the cup upside down on its saucer. When the final drop of tea has drained away, turn the cup the right way up again and begin your reading. Do not hurry. Give your imagination a chance to work. Turn the cup, tilt it, consider it from every angle. The clearer a symbol appears, the greater its importance. Do not, however, expect the images ever to be totally clear. Sometimes the leaves offer no more than a suggestion and it is up to you to interpret such hints. If you really cannot discern any pattern or symbol, tell your client the truth. Although you may allow yourself to add that the confusion of the leaves probably mirrors the state of mind.

Reading the symbols

The meaning of the various symbols is the most important thing. The list that follows gives some of the most commonly used, but your own imagination and, in time, experience, may lead you to add more of your own. The position and size of the symbols are also significant.

The client

The cup-handle represents the client. If a symbol is near the handle it indicates an occurrence close to the person's home. The direction taken by symbols which suggest movement is also important. Some will point to the handle, suggesting approach; and some away, suggesting departure. There is also one theory that, when holding the cup with the handle towards you, symbols to the left of the handle concern events in the past and those on the right events in the future.

Time

The sides of the cup, from rim to bottom, are taken as a time scale. Thus the position of the symbols is important: *near the rim* — they indicate events which will occur in the near future, *near the bottom* — events distant in time, *in the bottom* — ill-fortune at any time.

Proportion

The size of the symbol is also important, for example, the proportions of the symbol will give some indication of the size of the house your client might move to or the legacy he might receive.

Overall reading

First, consider which kind of symbols predominate and make a general assessment of good or bad fortune. This will give a logical structure to your reading. It will tell you whether any bad news the cup foretells will be no more than a minor blemish on a period of happiness, or whether the good will only lighten a bad period.

Remember that the message lies in the combination of all the symbols. Only when you have put them together will what they have to tell become clear.

If an ant and an eye, pointing to perseverance and watchfulness, are combined with a large and very clear gun near the cup's handle, this suggests that it is in the domestic arena that these qualities will be best deployed. If, however, the third symbol is a broken necklace, then the problems through which one has to persevere and over which one must watch arise from a love relationship. And an open book would translate the same effort into the legal field.

Every combination of signs has a different significance, making reading from cups a fairly exacting business, but also a rewarding one.

Left: This seems to be the cup of an unmarried person, for the horse's head on the right suggests that there is a lover in the offing — possibly a rich lover. Yet the head faces away, and that is not a good sign. There may be danger of a swift parting. Opposite the handle there stands a swaddled baby, indicative of a multiplicity of small worries, and the arrow-head which suggests that bad news is impending.

To the left, the signs indicate that a bad time has been passed through: a flying bat, pointing to the plots of false friends: the square, implying unwelcome restriction, and the jester's head which tells us that this situation was taken very seriously indeed.

Right: A period of domestic happiness has come to an end. In the past, to the left of the handle one finds the fish, a symbol of happiness, and a table, suggesting meetings, dinner parties and all manner of pleasant gatherings. But to the right of the handle, danger threatens: a hand grasps a gun, the muzzle toward the cup handle — domestic bliss is threatened, and very determinedly, by an outsider. (A gun can also indicate a call to arms.) Terror follows, for a devil-tailed monster leaps up from the disaster-cluttered bottom of the cup.

Meanings of the symbols

Acorns
An excellent symbol. The good fortune it foretells varies according to its position in the cup:
near the top — financial success
towards the middle — good health
near the bottom — improvement either in health or finances

Aircraft
A sudden journey, unexpected and not without risk
alternatively there will be a rise to new heights
if the aircraft seems broken — danger threatens, either physically or in one's career

Alligator
Treachery lies in wait

Anchor
Success awaits. Again the position in the cup is important:
at the top of the cup — success in business, augmented by the support of a faithful love
towards the middle — a voyage ending in prosperity (increased if dots surround the symbol)
at the bottom — good fortune socially. If the symbol is obscured — anticipate difficulties

Ant
With perseverance, success will arrive

Arc
Ill health threatens either career or

other plans, projects may be abandoned, accidents threaten

Arrow
Bad news is on the way

Axe
Difficulties face you, especially if only the axe-head appears

Baby
Many small worries threaten
alternatively, there may be an addition to the family

Bag
A trap awaits, likely to be successful if the bag is closed

Ball
Variable fortunes await you in life

Basket
A very good sign. Again pay attention to its position:
near the handle — a baby will soon be announced
near the top of the cup — your possessions will be added to
if flowers lie in the basket — a very good sign, suggesting happiness, social success, parties and festivities
if the basket is surrounded by dots — finances will be unexpectedly augmented, perhaps by a legacy

Bat
Beware of plots and of false friends

Bear
Irrational decisions will bring difficulties and even danger in their train
if the bear is turned away from the handle a long journey is indicated

Bed
if neat — a tidy mind
if disordered — an undisciplined mind which leads to problems

Bee
Success, both social and financial; good news
near the handle — a gathering of friends
a swarm of bees — possible success with an audience

Bell
News is expected, good or bad according to the significance of the surrounding symbols
near the top of the cup — promotion
near the bottom of the cup — sad news
two bells — great joy

Bird
This is particularly lucky if there are two or more birds
flying birds — good news
standing birds — a successful voyage

Boat
Refuge in time of trouble

Book
If the book is open expect litigation, if closed difficult researches

Boot
Protection from pain
pointing away from the handle
sudden removal, perhaps dismissal
broken — failure and disgrace threaten

Bottle
Take care of health

Bridge
Opportunity to be seized for short-cut to success

Broom
Small worries disappear

Butterfly
Frivolous but innocent pleasure
if surrounded by dots this indicates the frittering away of wealth

Cabbage
Jealousy entails complications

Candle
Helpfulness, zeal for education

Castle
Strong character, rising to position of authority

Cat
Someone lies in treacherous ambush, probably a false friend

Chair
Improvement and, if the chair is surrounded by dots, financial improvement

Circle
A successful outcome

Clock
Avoid delay and hesitation
alternatively — recovery from illness
in the bottom of the cup — a death

Clouds
Doubts, unsolved problems
if the clouds are very heavy, misfortune is indicated

Column
Success. Also a danger of resultant arrogance

Comet
A visitor from overseas

Cross
Suffering, sacrifice, tribulation. Two crosses indicate severe illness or other major affliction

Crown
Great success
If the crown is neat expect a legacy

Dagger
Impetuosity
alternatively — the dangerous plotting of enemies

Dog
Rely on friends
Pay attention to the position and attitude of the dog:
running — good news and happy meetings
subdued — you may be slandering a friend
at the bottom of the cup — a friend is in trouble

Dot

A single dot emphasizes the meaning of the symbol it is nearest to. Dots in groups indicate money

Drum

Scandal and gossip threaten. Quarrels are in the air.

Egg

Prosperity, success, fertility. The more eggs the better

Elephant

Wisdom, strength and slow, but solid, success

Eye

Take care and be watchful, especially in business

Feather

Instability and lack of concentration

Fence

Limitation imposed on plans and activities

Fern

Unfaithfulness is possible in a lover

Fir tree

Success, especially in the arts. The higher the tree the better

Fire

Avoid over-hasty reactions, especially anger

Fish

One of the very best omens, this indicates good luck in everything

Flag

Danger threatens, particularly if the flag is black

Flower

A wish will be granted

Fly

Worry, especially domestic. The more flies there are the more varied the swarm of misfortunes

Forked line

Decisions must be taken. (Whether these will be successful or not depends upon the attendant symbols)

Frog

Avoid self-importance as it may cause trouble

Fruit

This is a lucky symbol, especially if the fruit is in season

Garland

Success and great honour

Glass

Integrity

Goat

Enemies threaten

Gun

near the handle — an attack will threaten domestic happiness
at the bottom of the cup — slander undermines the client
for military personnel — cancelled leave

Hammer

Ability to overcome obstacles and perhaps a tendency to ruthlessness

Hare

Over-timidity

Harp

Domestic harmony
for single people a harp indicates a love affair with a successful outcome

Hat

New possibilities, and probable success
if the hat is bent and holed — failure is more likely
if the hat is in the bottom of the cup — a rival

Hawk

Sudden danger threatens

Hill

Obstacle to progress. (Especially if clouds obscure it)

Horse
galloping — good news, especially from a lover
the head only — a lover

House
Secure conditions, especially in business, so a good time for new ventures
if the sign is near the handle and obscured — domestic strife or illness may threaten the family

Human figures
Consider these carefully and take your cue from their appearance, activities and the surrounding symbols

Insect
Minor worries, soon overcome

Jester
Avoid frivolity, it might be a disadvantage. A time for seriousness

Jug
Influence, enabling the client to give help to another
near the handle — excellent health

Kettle
near the handle domestic contentment
near or at the bottom of the cup — domestic strife

Key
Intelligent appraisal can see and seize new opportunities
double, or near the bottom of the cup — danger of robbery

Knife
Separation, broken contracts, ended friendships
near the handle — divorce
crossed knives — bitter argument

Ladder
Promotion, probably through hard work

Leaf
News
if the leaves are in clusters — happiness and good fortune

Letter
News
if obscured —bad news
if near dots — news concerning financial affairs

Light-house
Trouble threatens but will be averted before it strikes

Lines
Progress, especially if clear and straight

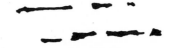

Lion
Influential friends and consequent success

Lock
Obstacle to your advancement

Man
near the handle — a visitor
with arms outstretched — bearing gifts

Mask
Take care, people are trying to deceive you

Mermaid
Take care, people are trying to tempt you

Monkey
Flatterers represent danger; they intend mischief

Monster
In any shape or form this indicates terror

Moon
full — a love affair
in first quarter — new projects
in last quarter — a decline in fortune
obscured — depression
surrounded by dots — marriage for money

Mountains
High ambition which will be successful if the peaks are very clear

Mushroom
Growth, expansion
near the handle — a new home in the country

Nail
Malice threatens and injustice may be inflicted

Necklace
complete — many supporters and admirers
broken — marriage or love affair may break up

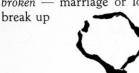

Net
Beware of traps

Nurse
Illness threatens
if near the handle — dependants may fall sick

Owl
This evil omen indicates that new ventures will fail
at the bottom of the cup — disease and financial failure
near the handle — unfaithfulness destroys domestic harmony

Palm
Success, honour and respect

Parachute
Escape from danger

Parcel
This is represented by an oblong leaf and indicates a surprise. (The surrounding symbols will offer a clue as to the nature of the surprise)

Parrot
Scandal and gossip threaten

Peacock
with tail spread — possession of an estate
surrounded by dots — a life of luxurious ease
near ring — a rich marriage

Pear
Comfort and financial ease

Pentagon
Mental and intellectual balance

Pig
Mixed fortune. (Material success may bring spiritual or psychological disaster)

Pistol
Danger, perhaps moral danger, threatens

Pot
Service to society

Profile
Temporary friendship, or acquaintanceship

Pump
A generous nature

Purse
Profit, usually material
at the bottom of the cup — this indicates an unexpected loss

Question mark
Hesitancy

Rabbit
Timidity

Rake
Attempts should be made to tidy things up and regulate life-style and work methods

Rat
Treachery and loss, deceitful friends and resourceful enemies

Reptile
Treachery and malice threaten, especially from false friends

Ring
Self-sufficiency, completion, eternity
near the top of the cup — a marriage is indicated
near the middle — marriage is offered
at the bottom — a long engagement (but if a cross is nearby it is doomed to be broken)
two rings — plans come to fruition, projects work out

Saw
Outsiders will theaten domestic tranquillity

Scales
A lawsuit is likely
balanced scales — justice will be done
unbalanced scales — injustice will be suffered

Scissors
Separation, quarrelling
near the handle — domestic bickering

Ship
Good fortune and/or good tidings are on their way

Skeleton
Ill health, poverty

Snake
Hatred and enmity, vicious plots

Spade
Hard work, but success at the end of it

Spider
This indicates a determined, persistent character (but with some guile and cunning)

Square
Restriction, even imprisonment: either external, of the body; or internal, of the mind

Sun
Great happiness, success and power

Star
six-pointed — good fortune
eight-pointed — a bad omen, accidents and reverses may be suffered
five stars — success, but no joy
seven stars — grief

Swallow
Swiftness of decision
This also indicates unexpected journeys, leading to a happy outcome

Swan
Smooth and contented life

Table
Dinner, party, feast, social gathering
dots nearby — a conference on financial matters

Toad
Beware of flattery and flatterers

Tortoise
Over-sensitivity to criticism

Trees
Plans will be fruitful, ambitions fulfilled

Triangle
pointing upwards — success
pointing downwards — plans go awry

Trunk
A journey and fateful decisions

Umbrella
Shelter will be needed
if the umbrella is open it will be found,
if closed, denied

Violin
Individualism, perhaps egoism

Volcano
Passions may erupt and cause harm

Vulture
Loss, perhaps through theft; danger, possibly from an enemy in authority

Whale
Pre-eminence and success, especially in business

Windmill
Success will be achieved through industry and hard work, not brilliance

Wings
News is expected. (The attendant symbols will suggest whether this will be good or bad)

Woman
Happiness and pleasure
more than one woman, scandal and gossip

Yoke
Domination threatens, so avoid being too submissive

Zebra
Adventures overseas. (An unsettled life is indicated)

Dice

These deceptively simple little cubes with numbers marked upon them have been held to be responsible for making and breaking men's fortunes. The random nature of Fate is believed to be nowhere more clearly expressed than in the throwing of dice. Every throw is apparently completely unpredictable. The Egyptians knew these ancient toys, so did the Greeks. And throughout Asia precious woods and metals were used to make them in order to add to their latent power.

Method of reading

Dice have been used for divination for thousands of years, and methods of reading them have passed through many variations. There are, however, two absolute rules. For divination there must be three numbered dice, and they must be thrown in complete silence. It is also generally believed that they run more freely when the weather is calm and the atmosphere cool.

The most common method is to draw a simple chalk circle on a table and then throw the dice on behalf of the person whose fortune you are telling. Dice that roll beyond the circle have nothing to say. Those that fall on the floor indicate that disturbed and vexing times are ahead, which will probably be darkened by quarrels. If all the dice roll out of the circle, they should be picked up and thrown again. However, should the second throw also yield no result, it might be as well to assume that Fate has nothing to communicate that day, and wait until a more propitious moment.

There are two general points to remember. If a number turns up more than once during a reading, it presages the arrival of significant news. And on the very rare occasions when one dice lands on top of another it is always a warning that extreme caution should be exercised in all commercial and romantic ventures.

Meaning of numbers

Once the three dice have been rolled, add together the numbers shown on them. If one has rolled outside the circle and the total is less than three, the dice have nothing to say. The list which follows gives the most familiar meanings of the total numbers.

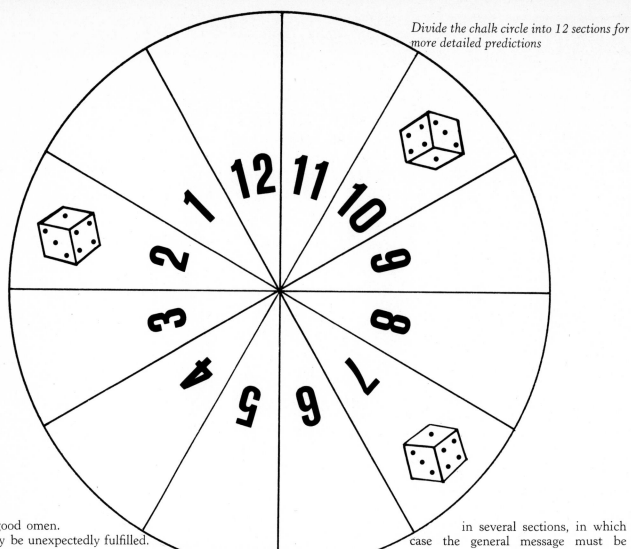

Divide the chalk circle into 12 sections for more detailed predictions

Three A good omen.
A wish may be unexpectedly fulfilled.
Four Disappointment
Five A stranger will bring joy
Six Material loss from which some spiritual advantage may be gained
Seven Unfounded gossip will cause unhappiness
Eight A contemplated action has not been thought through, and may produce an injustice
Nine Success, particularly in amorous affairs. If there has been a quarrel, expect reunion, forgiveness, reconciliation
Ten Domestic contentment, and perhaps some professional or business advancement
Eleven Someone — not necessarily a member of the family or close friend — is ill
Twelve A letter will come, and an answer be demanded. Ask advice before coming to a decision
Thirteen Grief, probably protracted, perhaps even lifelong
Fourteen A stranger will become a close and dear friend
Fifteen Temptation to enter into a shady or unjust deal
Sixteen A journey. Take it, for it will pass pleasantly and end in profit
Seventeen A man from overseas, prob-ably a foreigner, will suggest a course of action to you. His suggestion will be sound
Eighteen A very good omen — promotion, profit and joy

Specific predictions

In order to make predictions more precise, you may divide the chalk circle into twelve parts. These twelve sections represent the following:
First section Next year's happenings
Second section Money matters
Third section Travel
Fourth section Domestic matters
Fifth section Present schemes
Sixth section Health
Seventh section Marriage
Eighth section Deaths — and legacies
Ninth section Present state of mind
Tenth section Work or profession
Eleventh section Friends
Twelfth section Enemies
Continue to take notice of the general message, read as above, offered by the three dice added together, and apply this to the particular sections in which the dice fall. They will probably fall in several sections, in which case the general message must be combined with those yielded by the separate sections. If two or three dice fall into one section this, of course strengthens the message they offer. The numbers on the individual dice are read as follows:
One Search whatever the dice say about this matter for indications of success
Two Success depends on friendly relations continuing
Three Success is bound to follow
Four Things will go badly, as far as this section's affairs are concerned
Five The indications are good
Six The problem under general discussion will in its outcome have a good effect on the matter covered by this particular section
There are no hard-and-fast rules about giving an overall prediction under this more specific method. The general message offered by the three dice must somehow be combined with the particular ones from the individual sections. Use your subtlety and intuition to bring this sometimes fragmented and almost incoherent information into an ordered and relevant meaning. It will be enjoyable to discover how much skill you have.

Dominoes

The pieces used in the game of dominoes can, like dice, reveal possible expressions of the operations of Fate. Here the diviner shuffles the pieces, face downwards, and draws one on behalf of the client. The piece is turned upwards and read according to the table below. It is then returned, face down, to the rest of the pieces, which again are shuffled. A second piece is then drawn and read. This operation may be repeated for a third time, but no more. If one draws more than three pieces at a consultation, or allows more than one consultation per person a day, the dominoes become tired and are liable to mislead you!

Meanings

Double Six Success in every way
Six/Five Charitable works
Six/Four Litigation which is unlikely to be successful
Six/Three Short voyage with a beneficial outcome
Six/Two A gift, likely to be useful and to be presented soon
Six/One An end to the root of all your troubles

Six/Blank Be careful — especially with those you think are your friends
Double Five A move to a new house or apartment, where happiness awaits
Five/Four Profits. But do not use these for speculative ventures
Five/Three A helpful visitor
Five/Two A child is born, probably within the subject's family
Five/One Love affair — passionate but ending unhappily
Five/Blank Give comfort to a friend in trouble
Double Four A party given by a stranger
Four/Three Expected disappointments need not be feared
Four/Two A swindler — perhaps a philanderer — has entered the client's life
Four/One Debts must be paid — even at risk of temporary poverty
Four/Blank Attempt reconcilliation with estranged friend
Double Three A rival in love. Distress and misery result.
Three/Two Avoid tempting fortune for a few days
Three/One Surprising news, of great usefulness
Three/Blank Jealousy makes trouble and disrupts friendship
Double Two Happy marriage
Two/One Loss of money or property, this to occur in the very near future

Two/Blank Meeting, a new relationship and consequent happiness
Double One Avoid hesitation; a bold decision awaits and should be taken
One/Blank A stranger, probably from overseas, who will be of use
Double Blank A bad omen — indication of loss, disappointment, unhappiness

Sometimes you will draw the same piece twice. This confirms the prediction and at the same time suggests it will happen very soon. Usually however, as so often with predictions, the dominoes offer fragments of information which you yourself must build into a coherent message.

Take as much care and time as you need in order to organize the diverse clues into a clear picture. Concentrate hard. Imagination and those latent psychic powers may very well help you to a surprising degree of accuracy.

Reading

The client is a middle-aged housewife, and Five/Four, Four/One and Six/Two are drawn in that order (see picture below), showing that she will receive a windfall. However, she will have to use it to meet old bills. To take away the sting of that, a present will arrive — which may or may not be all the better for being a useful one.

Phrenology: reading the bumps on the head

Throughout the eighteenth and nineteenth centuries, European scientists were dominated by an urge to classify. They named and separated into groups every creature and object in Nature that they could discover — and human beings were no exception.

It was felt there must be a hidden key by means of which every man or woman could be graded into a specific category. And if this key could only be found society would automatically become rational, tidy and controlled. Those with administrative abilities would enter the civil service, the courageous would become military men, the imaginative would be creative artists, and so on. All that was needed was an instant method of analyzing character.

One of the methods which was tested was phrenology — the interpretation of the bumps on people's skulls. This is now somewhat discredited as a science although it still has its adherents. You need not, however, accept it in its entirety — or even at all — in order to have fun with it: it makes an intriguing icebreaker at a party!

Origins

The man who founded it, a German doctor named Gall, was extremely serious about it. He concluded that the brain was the controlling organ of the body, the seat of the mind, and that different parts of it had special functions. Because the brain lay under the skull and the skull was irregularly shaped, with shallow lumps and hollows which varied from one person to another, Gall argued that the size of these bumps revealed the development, or lack of it, of that part of the brain which lay immediately beneath. If one knew what faculties corresponded to those areas of the brain, one would be able to evaluate character merely by a careful examination of a person's skull.

Having decided how parts of the brain and particular characteristics corresponded, Gall, and an assistant named Spurzheim, persisted in the work of spreading their doctrine and, although they died largely unrecognized and unaccepted, their ideas continued slowly to gain in popularity throughout the nineteenth century. In Britain this happened mainly through the work of a Scotsman named George Combe.

Method

Because your client has to sit very still, the more quickly you can read the bumps, the better. It is helpful to practise first on yourself, and then on any patient friend who can be persuaded to keep still for long enough. First, study the head and features of your subject as a whole. Then, gently, but with the fingertips quite firm against the scalp, feel the contours of the skull, moving across the head in a systematic way.

Remember that there are no absolutes in phrenology. What matters is not how large or small a particular bump may be in itself, but how it compares with the others. It is the prominence of one characteristic against the rest which you are trying to determine.

Meaning of bumps

Combe's *System of Phrenology* listed 37 significant areas of the brain. In each, he stated, was based a particular trait of character which could be discerned by the corresponding bump on the skull. Since the brain has two lobes, each characteristic is represented by two bumps, one on each side of the head. Thus both hands can be used simultaneously in the attempt to discern them.

The four groups

Combe divided the bumps into four groups. The first revealed the basic propensities or qualities of the client. The second corresponded to his sentiments or feelings. The third corresponded to perception. And the fourth group referred to what were called the reflective areas, indicating reason and the mental processes by which we order our knowledge.

The following is a breakdown of the meanings given to the bumps in each area. Check the precise positions of these against the diagram.

Qualities

1. Sexuality If too small, this bump indicates a lack of energy, perhaps even of balance. If too large, it suggests so great an interest in the opposite sex as to prove a handicap — unless it is sublimated, turning the person to religious or charitable works.

2. Self-preservation If very small this indicates possible suicidal tendencies. A relatively small bump suggests recklessness, certainly some disregard for personal safety. A correspondingly large one points to a disinclination to take risks, sometimes amounting to cowardice.

3. Parenthood The larger the bump, the more deeply implanted will be a maternal or paternal instinct.

4. Domesticity Those with a gipsy mentality will probably not show a developed bump in this area. It relates to the delights of staying at home, and people who have it will tend to be faithful to their spouse and their firesides.

5. Friendship This bump displays the qualities of loyalty and trustworthiness we look for in friends.

6. Competitiveness Beware of those who have an over-development of this bump, for they will prove quarrelsome and petulant. If the development is only fairly large, however, such people will have a tendency to push for what they want or believe to be right. A lack of it would be a poor indication of success in careers.

7. Impatience If too large, it suggests destructive traits, a measure of harshness. In moderate size it points to a refusal to tolerate unnecessary impediments and obstacles.

8. Secretiveness Too small a bump here points to insensitive and brutal honesty. Too large a one, to a tendency to conceal and lie. In proportion, however, it suggests tact.

9. Acquisitiveness In a competitive, commercial society this is, perhaps, not a bad quality to have. But if the bump is too large, it hints at hoarding, miserliness and even, in extreme cases, to a tendency to take what is not one's own.

10. Appetite Well-developed, this suggests a discriminating palate. Over-developed, a tendency to gluttony. But under-developed, a lack of vitality and of taste.

11. Achievement This relates to the ability to make or create, whether manually or in the arts or sciences. Too small a bump is a poor indication for success in life. Too large a one suggests the subject will attempt more than he can manage.

Feelings

12. Self-esteem This bump should be easily discernible, but in balance, avoiding indications of vainglory on the one hand, or inferiority feelings on the other.

13. Approbativeness This indicates the wish to do well either in private pursuits or in a career. Too large a bump may indicate vanity and an inflated self-importance, while a small one shows a disregard for society's opinion.

14. Prudence Too large a bump points to over-caution, while a deficiency indicates foolish recklessness.

15. Benevolence Too small a bump indicates a mean and selfish nature, but too large a one points to a mindless, universal charity.

16. Respect This indicates respect for those who deserve it, and perhaps veneration in the religious sense. One that is too large points to an unpleasantly subservient nature, and perhaps religous mania; too small, to a possibly undisciplined revolutionary zeal.

17. Determination This is self-explanatory. But be aware of the possibility of over-development sufficient to indicate obstinacy and unreasonableness.

18. Conscientiousness Again, this is self-explanatory but over-development of this bump could lead to inferiority feelings and a constant sense of guilt.

19. Optimism Too large a bump suggests a credulous person.

20. Belief Too large a bump indicates the fanatic, the acceptor of all superstitions; too small, the sceptic.

21. Beauty A bump denoting ability to appreciate the beautiful, whether in nature or in art. If too large, it can suggest dissatisfaction with the everyday.

22. Humour Self-explanatory. Those who have this bump well-developed are liable to turn their wit caustically on those whom they disapprove. Better that, perhaps, than the solemnity displayed by those in whom this bump is under-developed.

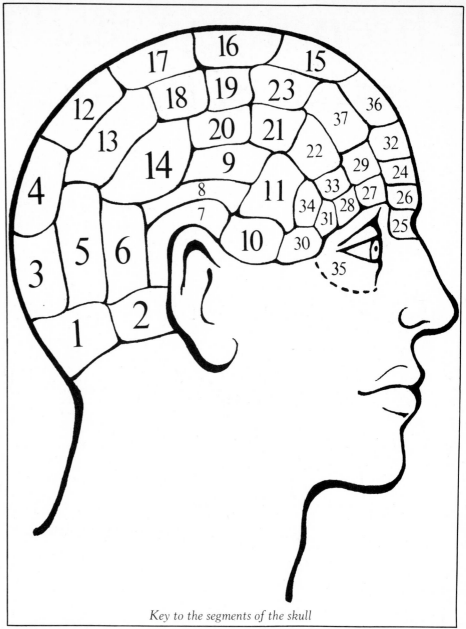

Key to the segments of the skull

23. Emulation This is allied to the ability to learn, so it is especially useful in the young. But if too large it denotes a certain lack of self-assertion.

Perception

24. Observation This denotes the general ability to differentiate between one thing and another, to take in one's environment. If too large, it suggests the spy and the gossip.

25. Shape If well-developed, this bump suggests high mathematical ability, awareness of shape and form and a good memory for them.

26. Size This bump denotes the ability to perceive and evaluate the relative importance of things, not only physically, but in events as well. Architects and draughtsmen will do well if they have such a bump.

27. Weight An understanding of mechanical forces is suggested by this, pointing to balance, both physical and

mental and perhaps some athletic skill.

28. Colour Self-explanatory. This will be developed in painters and country lovers.

29. Place memory Again, self explanatory. Well-developed this bump suggests the eager traveller.

30. Numbers Calculating skill, arithmetical dexterity.

31. Orderliness An understanding of sequence and regularity is denoted here. But in excess, this bump hints at overtidiness and fussiness over details.

32. Memory for events This bump points to a really good memory, particularly for events in the client's personal history, or in history generally. Thus it is a bump denoting a successful student.

33. Time sense A bump indicating an acute sense of time, and thus probably of rhythm. Connected with possible musical ability.

34. Melody Denoting a strong sense of harmony, this bump would confirm

any musical ability indicated by the previous one.

35. Verbal expression A dexterity with words is indicated here. It may be literary, oratorical or linguistic, depending on other characteristics.

Reason

36. Comparison This bump stands for a most important analytical faculty: the one which allows us to compare and contrast objects, events, items of information, ideas and plans.

37. Causality This bump, if developed, suggests logical skill. The ability to argue backwards to first principles, forwards to a rational conclusion. These traits suggest the philosopher, theologian or author.

Analysis

You must always remember that these

bumps are not very high, nor very clearly defined. To discover them takes a fair amount of practice. The skull is like a landscape, one feature flowing into another, and to identify each one by touch alone is not easy. If the minor variations in personality are more difficult to discover, you should nevertheless attempt to do so, for the main traits of character are greatly modified by those less important elements which cluster about them. Here again, the information given by the shape and varying thickness of the skull reaches you through the fingers item by item. It is up to you to combine those items into an overall analysis.

For example, a large bump of Self-esteem, a large bump of Benevolence, a small bump of Acquisitiveness, allied to a large lump of Friendship and a small bump of Domesticity, particularly if there is a well-developed bump of

Phrenology was part of the nineteenth-century popular theatre — here 'the Great Baggs' is seen lecturing during a scene from 'Apple Blossoms' at the Vaudeville Theatre.

Appetite, adds up to a character picture which may well be that of a man who spends his evenings buying drinks for everyone, getting his satisfaction from being liked for his material generosity to his friends. But other bumps may modify this picture. Bumps of Conscientiousness, of Humour, of Causality, could materially alter the analysis, and reveal a rather more complex and intelligently thoughtful character.

It is your understanding and intuitive sense which must put everything together to create a final picture, both consistent and accurate, from the contours of your client's head.

Numerology: what numbers reveal

Numbers stand for order. With mathematics a complex problem can be reduced to numerical terms and arrive at a logical conclusion. Because of this, because numbers can bring order out of apparent chaos, people have always attempted to manipulate numbers and use their power to unravel the complexities of human personality and life. Numbers therefore appear in many different ways and in several methods of fortune-telling. The varied Kabbalistic theologians, both of antiquity and the Middle Ages, used numbers, in association with a curious alphabet which was part Hebrew and part Greek, for divination. The Babylonians, skilled astronomers and mathematicians as well as astrologers, magicians and soothsayers, believed that numbers had secrets to reveal. And astrologers in general have always relied on numbers to an extent. Clearly they had to as calculations based on the hour and date of a person's birth played such a large part in their analyses. The methods of analysis which follow are simple and amusing to use. Even if you are a poor mathematician you can use numerology, the 'science' of numbers, to gain some insights into the characters of those around you — and into your own character, too.

Primary numbers

The numbers are each linked to a planet, and it is the planet which suggests the major characteristics associated with the number.

One
The Sun Ambition, action, even aggression; but also creativity, individuality and the positive elements in character.

Two
The Moon Imagination, receptivity,

Each number — usually so ordinary — can have a mysterious power of its own, an individual atmosphere.

artistic qualities; also balance and harmony.

Three
Jupiter Authority, conscientiousness, a strong sense of duty. Because this number also stands for the trinity it shows attachment to the family.

Four
Uranus Opposition, rebellion, reform. These traits are often coupled with idealism and a lack of worldly success.

Five
Mercury Excitable, highly strung, always searching for new adventures.

Six
Venus Attractive, even magnetic, with a love of beauty; easy to make friends with, trusting and to be trusted.

Seven
Neptune Love of travel. This is also the magic number so it stands for psychic powers.

Eight
Saturn Intensity and loneliness, extremism. This often indicates great success but at some cost to private happiness.

Nine
Mars Determination, will, aggression, a hastiness of temper, both courage and impulsiveness. This is the most important of the single numbers and is thought of as having great power.

Secondary numbers

Compound numbers also have their significance, and there are several ways of determining the appropriate number and deciding what it means. In one system, the significant numbers run from 10 to 52, and are arrived at by simply adding together the values of all the letters in either the given or family name of the enquirer.
Another system, below, remembering that the Hebrew alphabet has twenty-

two characters and that Numerology has Kabbalistic associations, considers only the numbers from 10 to 22 as meaningful. In this system it is the second given name, the one which is not normally used, which is coded into numbers. The numbers have the meanings given below.
Ten Attainment, self-confidence, completion.
Eleven Success. But there are hidden dangers, threats of treachery.

Twelve Uncertainty, anxiety, repression, even victimization.
Thirteen Neither lucky nor unlucky. This number is, however, symbolic of power which wrongly used can bring destruction, not least upon the user.
Fourteen Danger overcome, especially natural hazards.
Fifteen Obstinacy, strength of personality, verbal facility.
Sixteen Accident, danger — hence a warning, especially to the over-confident, who need to take more care.
Seventeen Harmony, spirituality.
Eighteen A warning of quarrels and a destructive materialism. Its very association with materialism can, however, mean that it adds strength to what the primary numbers suggest, supporting the good, providing a counterweight to the bad.
Nineteen Good fortune, inspiration, success, new and brilliant ideas.
Twenty Of doubtful influence, suggesting on the one hand zest for new plans; on the other, steadiness in

carrying them out—a steadiness perhaps not strong enough to restrain the impetuous.

Twenty-one Ambition achieved, freedom, independence; but in those whose Primary number is 3, it suggests overconfidence, impatience.

Twenty-two A strong number, increasing the significance of what the Primary number has indicated. It suggests dreams and false judgements, so it may lead to disaster.

Date of birth

In numerology, as in astrology, the subject's date of birth is important. This is to be expected as it is a personal set of numbers relating to the day on which he or she was born.

This date is simply converted to a Primary number. Just write the whole birth date out in figures, add them together once, then add together the result, until you are left with only a single figure. So, if the client was born on April 14th, 1945, the date in figures is 4.14.1945, which you write as the sum, $4+1+4+1+9+4+5$. The answer, 28 gives you the sum $2+8$, which in turn gives you the answer 10. And that, added together, gives the single number you need for the reading — the number 1.

Names

To give a deeper character analysis apply the divinatory power of numbers to the client's name and surname.

Numerical equivalents
This simple key gives a numerical equivalent for each letter.

A B C D E F G H I

J K L M N O P Q R

S T U V W X Y Z

1 2 3 4 5 6 7 8 9

Using this method the name 'Janet', for example, becomes 11552. Proceeding in the usual way this becomes the sum, $1+1+5+5+2=14$. These two figures added together give you the Primary number 5.

Numbers have always had ritual significance, especially in the religions that are based on the Bible. Left top: the Seven Angels bearing plague; bottom left: the Four Horsemen of the Apocalypse; bottom right: the Second Coming of Christ.

Follow exactly the same method to reduce a surname to a Primary number. However, when dealing with the second given name, omit the final stage because for this Secondary number you need a double figure.

When the second given name is too short or has too many A's to give a double figure, use 10 as an equivalent for 1, 11 for 2, 12 for 3, etc. Do the same when the name adds up to more than 22; that is, reduce it to a Primary, then find the double-figure equivalent. So, for example, if the name adds up to the figure 32, that would reduce to the single number 5, which gives you the Secondary number 14.

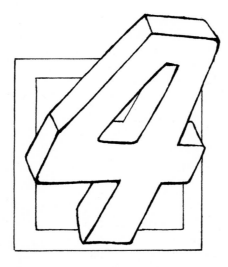

Cheiro's system

Cheiro, the famous French clairvoyant and palmist who lived and worked in the late nineteenth century, gives in his *Book of Numbers* a key which he claims may have originated with the Chaldeans. (Alphabets have changed so much since then that this is difficult to prove or disprove.) Here is his version.

A—1	G—3	N—5	T—4
B—2	H—5	O—7	U—6
C—3	I/J-1	P—8	V—6
D—4	K—2	Q—1	W—6
E—5	L—3	R—2	X—5
F—8	M—4	S—3	Y—1
	Z—7		

A full analysis

Once you have mastered the use of the keys and the meanings of the numbers you can give someone a full reading. To do this you reduce the client's birth-date, name and surname to Primary numbers. These, reduced again to a Primary number, give you the Character number — the key to the client's character. The client's second,

less-used, given name is reduced to a Secondary number and this tells you which character traits are strengthened or weakened.

Suppose, for example, that you have to analyze the character and prospects of a lady named Mary Pamela Waters, who tells you she was born on September 15, 1951. Following the procedure above her birthdate is reduced to the sum $9+1+5+1+9+5+1=31=4$.

Next ask her whether she is normally called Mary or Pamela. This will tell you which name gives you the Primary and which the Secondary influences. If it is 'Mary' which she most often uses, write that name and the name 'Waters' vertically, one below the other, then write beside the letters their equivalents in figures.

Using the first of the two keys above (not Cheiro's system), this would give you the following:

M=4
A=1
R=9
Y=7
Total: 21=2+1=
Primary number 3
W=5
A=1
T=2
E=5
R=9
S=1
Total: 23=2+3=
Primary number 5

Thus: total name number is $3+5=8$
birth date number is 4
—
Total=12
Thus: $1+2=$Character number 3

You now know that the main characteristics of Mary Waters are those associated with the number Three: conscientiousness, a strong sense of duty, an authoritarian streak. To find out to what extent these traits are modified turn to her less-used middle name. Using the same key this gives you:

P=7
A=1
M=4
E=5
L=3
A=1 Total: 21=Secondary number.

You discover that Mary's already strong personality is given even more force by her secondary characteristics: her individuality, her need for independence. In all, this analysis suggests that she will be a very successful woman, although her personal relationships might suffer.

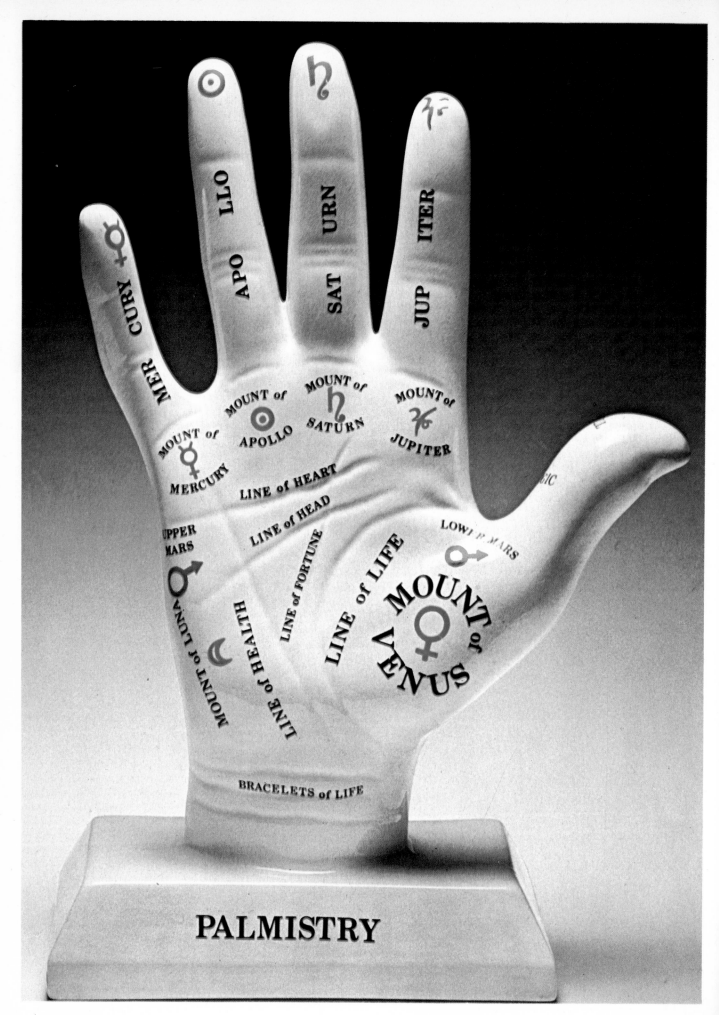

PALMISTRY

Palmistry: reading the hands

There are two aspects to palmistry. The first, called Chirognomy, attempts from the shape of the hand to analyze a person's psychological and emotional make-up. The second, Chiromancy, seeks to use the lines of the hand to foretell a person's future. Palmistry is very old. It was known in China over five thousand years ago, and some people think that it began there. Others believe that it was first practised either in Egypt or India.

Reading of hands is still widespread in modern India, and throughout the Middle East too. The Ancient Greeks knew of it — Aristotle certainly mentioned it, calling the hand 'the organ of organs'. It was known in Western Europe at an early stage, too. The first datable use of the word 'palmistry' was in a book written in English in the fifteenth century, but since books were rare at that time and seldom survived, it was probably used long before.

It is hard to be certain whether the lines of the palm actually foretell the future. That they, and the shape and structure of the hand, should give an indication of character is, however, much more plausible. From the literature on the subject, one can believe that some sort of connection has been more or less proved. Thus an analytical reading is likely to be more accurate, more useful and, in some ways, even more amusing than speculative prognostications of an uncertain future. Not only that: it cannot be repeated too often that such prognostications carry their own dangers. People tend to be credulous in these matters, nor need you believe that they are not when they protest their scepticism. Prophecies may, therefore, prove worrying for them and, in some cases, may alter their attitudes and plans.

Thus the palmist, however temporary and amateur, has responsibilities and should be aware of them and be very careful in the way they are discharged. A cautious silence is wiser than reckless forecasts of disturbing events.

Hand prints

A superficial reading of a hand can be done fairly quickly, but anything more detailed requires time. For this reason, and because it provides you with examples to study and learn from, it is a good plan to take prints of palms you want to examine. If you do this, anyone whose hand you decide to study does not have to sit still for the length of time that it takes to obtain a complete reading. This also has its uses when you want to read the hand of a child. The lines in the palms of children begin to be of significance during the first year — an age when they are not renowned for their willingness to keep still!

For a hand print you will need ink of the kind used in lino-cuts, a five-inch roller, a sheet of glass and a rubber pad not less than twelve inches square. Cover the roller in the ink, then roll it out on the glass to give it an even coating. Then ink the hand you want to examine. Try to cover it as evenly as possible. Have a sheet of good-quality heavy white paper ready on the rubber pad and press the hand to it, making sure that it does not slide sideways and so blur the impression. For the same reason, hold the paper firmly when the hand is raised from the paper. To start with, you may have to make several impressions before you have one good enough to use, but in a little while you will gain in confidence and skill.

There is another quick method, if you have access to certain types of flat copying machine. You can obtain a very good print in a few seconds, simply by laying your hand on the glass plate and operating the machine in the usual way. Care should be taken not to press the palm on the glass as this can obscure the lines. The samples given later in this chapter show how good the results can be.

For a time, most of the palms you examine will look strange and uninformative, but in time, like an explorer, you will learn how to fill in the blank parts of the map. For practice, you may be tempted to use your own palms, but in many ways this is unsatisfactory. We know ourselves — or we think we do. As a result, if we examine our own palms what we see must pass through that mesh of preconceptions, both flattering, and unflattering, that all of us have about ourselves. The habit of clear thought comes better from concentrating on the palms of other people. This is one reason why the ink and roller are so important.

Types of hand

Once you have the print — clear and yours to examine at leisure — what do you actually look for? First, apply the principles of chirognomy and consider the shape of the hand; the shape, length and placing of the fingers; and the position and prominence of the various mounds. This will enable you to assess the character of the subject. Take your time over this.

There are various ways of dividing the types of hand, but basically hands are either square or long.

Square hand

The square hand is one in which square fingers stem strongly from a square palm. This formation indicates practicality, a sense of order, a certain caution. People with square hands are generally practical, with their feet firmly on the ground. Their reliability will make them true friends and faithful lovers. Their liking for hard work, honesty and strength of purpose help them to do well in tasks that require physical effort. Their practicality and application are always indicated by the squareness of the palm, regardless of the length or shape of the fingers.

Long hand

The long hand, also called the conic or the artistic hand, usually has a slightly tapering palm, wider nearer the wrist, narrower at the base of the fingers. The fingers, too, taper gradually to rounded, cone-like tips. As a rule, such hands have small thumbs, and these indicate an impulsive temperament that can be inconstant. People with long hands tend to be very open to external influences and can become infatuated, with ideas and places as much as with people. Their moods can fluctuate between enthusiasm and dejection. Generous and sympathetic, they take up causes, sometimes of a revolutionary nature. They can be furious, but rarely for long, and they are not given to prolonged sulking. Because of the intensity of their feelings, they tend to pursue careers in the arts.

However, a hand that is too long and delicate can suggest that the depth of feelings may be greater than the staying power. For the artist, a better hand-shape might be tapering fingers rooted in a square and practical palm, or a long palm with square-ended fingers. Both these shapes promise a mixture of sensitivity and hard work which can lead to success.

Mixed characteristics

The subject of mixed hands is important in practical terms because not all hands conform to the theoretical purity of types.

Short fingers and long palm This combination suggests energy, speed of reaction, activity — especially if the palm is covered with many fine lines. But it also suggests impatience with the slower and less energetic. A person with this impatience may be somewhat at the mercy of his own versatility and there can be no doubt about his stability and reliability. People with hands of this type tend to choose individualistic, even unconventional occupations, certainly those which offer a variety of challenges and demand flair as much as application.

Long fingers and square palm The combination of long fingers and square palm is found in people who prefer reason to emotion, order to chaos. Such people put a possibly exaggerated emphasis on theory, on how things ought to be, without making enough allowance for how things actually are, influenced by human frailty, feelings and idiosyncracies. The work they choose, however, will usually be interesting and they will often show originality in it. They are, above all, the people to call on in problem situations. They may be teachers, journalists, even philosophers. Certainly they are often found in work that involves communication in one form or another.

Spatulate fingers Some hands, either long or short, have fingers shaped like spatulas, wider in the top segment than lower down. Sometimes their palms are of the same shape. This hand is usually a sign of great originality, combined with self-confidence and, often, creative energy, a mixture of qualities that is not suited to the solitude of a scholarly or artistic life. It is more likely to make people tend towards an outdoor life — an engineer, an explorer, or a successful soldier, for example, might have a palm and fingers of this shape. Some hands are truly mixed. Their fingers — short, long and spatulate — seem to have been brought together from various types of hand. When the mixture is marked, it points to a person of great versatility, someone who might also find it difficult to keep to one goal.

Other general features

Size of hand

There is also the size of the hand to be considered. Large hands suggest a reflective temperament, the ability to take stock before arriving at decisions. Small hands often belong to people who have a swift, intuitive awareness of the characters of those they meet, and of any decisions that must be taken, but who dislike finicky detail or laborious caution. They think big and act fast, and their haste can sometimes create problems for them.

Knotty joints

Knotty joints on the fingers suggest neatness, exactness, a power to observe and concentrate. They are said to be especially common on the hands of scientists.

Texture and elasticity

Make a note, too, of the texture of the skin of the hand you are studying. Fine skin can be a sign of sensitivity. When the skin of the hand is elastic and resistant it can be taken as an indication of energy and willpower. However, if the skin is very hard, this may suggest obstinacy and a lack of perception.

Flexibility

You may also take manual flexibility as an indication of mental flexibility, taking into account the age and occupation of the person whose hand you are studying.

The thumb

When you have come to a decision about the overall character of the hand, it is time to consider some of the details. First of these is the thumb, indicative of energy, symbol of the vital forces within us. A large thumb, therefore, suggests an energetic personality, making a forceful impact on the world.

The top, or nail, segment of the thumb, if it is particularly large, suggests a developed and powerful will and a great deal of staying-power. When this segment is rather narrow — and particularly if it is slightly pointed — the indication is of energies being uncontrolled and wasted.

The second segment, related to logic and reason, is sometimes markedly thinner than the top one, and this can indicate impulsiveness and a lack of control, a tendency to act hastily on impulse. Conversely, a thick, well-developed second segment suggests good control — even too high a degree

of it, great reasoning powers and consequent caution.

Consider, too, the relative lengths of the two thumb segments in order to see what balance there may be between energy and reason. When the thumb is set low in the hand, the energy it expresses is likely to be held back.

The fingers

Index finger

Since it is closest to the thumb, the index finger — or 'finger of Jupiter' — is often considered in conjunction with it. Also called 'the finger of ambition', it indicates the kind of desires for which the energy indicated by the thumb will be available and their strength.

A long index finger This suggests the desire to dominate and ambitiousness. If the energy of the thumb supports the ambition, the latter can result in a successful life, although not necessarily in a happy or well-adjusted one. If the energy indicated by the thumb is weak, however, then desire is likely to outreach grasp and this will result in feelings of failure and inadequacy.

Short index finger This, too, suggests feelings of inadequacy. When the finger belongs to a hand indicating a high degree of sensitivity, you can assume that you are studying someone retiring, meek and possibly put upon by others.

Straight index finger If the finger is straight this is a sign of well developed powers of observation, which will not be present if the finger is bent.

Curved index finger An index finger which bends towards the middle finger is a sign of a tendency to hoard and hold on to money. It shows a general lack of openness towards the outside world.

Middle finger

The middle finger, considered to be under the influence of Saturn, is a good indication of overall psychological balance. A long middle finger can be a sign of an over-intellectual approach to life. Conversely, a short middle finger indicates impulsiveness, a tendency to act on inner promptings rather than on a cool consideration of reality. The heavier and more dominating the finger, the more clearly it indicates seriousness and thoughtfulness. If the middle section is markedly larger than the other two, this indicates a love of the

Right: an intriguing and romantic party game — reading the palm of your favourite man.

country and of gardening.

Ring finger

This, the 'finger of Apollo', relates to the emotions and the better its shape and over-all balance, the steadier the psychological balance of the subject is likely to be. If the finger seems out of proportion with the rest of the hand, this may be a sign of an emotional life out of phase with the rest of the subject's existence. A very short finger, for example, can indicate difficulties in adjusting to other people, individual-istic solutions to emotional problems, a nature given to arousing and even provoking conflict with others. A longer finger than expected points to a high degree of introversion and pre-occupation with oneself and one's inner needs.

Little finger

The little finger, dedicated to Mercury, should be looked at in conjunction with the ring finger, the finger of Apollo, for it gives an indication of how well people are able to get on with others. Most important is its placing. If it is isolated from the other fingers, it indicates an inability to relate to other people and to form attachments. A long top segment to the little finger

suggests fluency with words. If the finger as a whole appears a little twisted it can indicate untruthfulness.

Nails

The fingernails also have their sig-nificance. When they are short and broad with square tips, they indicate a high level of irritability and some degree of obstinacy. Short nails which are slightly rounded, however, suggest energy and a developed, even intru-sive, curiosity. The long, oval nails of the dandy or the languid beauty in-dicate, as one might expect, no great energy, but a certain tolerance and an easygoing nature. They also show a high level of idealism and people interested in mysticism may well have nails of this kind. The larger the moons, the healthier the heart is likely to be. When the rest of the nail is very red in colour, the subject is likely to have a quick fierce temper. Better red nails than very pale, white ones perhaps, for the latter are thought to denote selfishness.

Palm contours : the mounts

Now look at the palm of the hand and the pads of flesh which give it its

variations in contour. These are called the mounts.

The Mount of Venus

This lies between wrist and thumb and indicates energy. When it is fleshy and high, energy is strong and needs to be expressed physically rather than through thought or feeling. People with this form of mount, therefore, are often at their best working with their hands and muscles, particularly if they have a square-palmed, square-fingered hand. Alternatively they will tend to be very active sexually, although whether with one partner or with many only the rest of the hand can indicate. A well-developed Mount of Venus also suggests a high level of artistic ability, particularly when it is crossed by lines running towards the thumb from the Life Line.

The Mount of the Moon

Opposite the Mount of Venus, directly below the end of the Head Line, this also indicates energy, the energy of the imagination, which can feed creativity, although it does not guarantee it. In fact, when this mount extends well down the wrist, it suggests a sensitivity so extreme that it may inhibit all artistic work. But on a square hand,

a well developed Mount of the Moon indicates imagination controlled by practicality, consequently it can indicate success in such careers as architecture or journalism. However, study of the rest of the hand may show that the imagination is uncontrolled and expressed in day-dreaming rather than definite action. The qualities of the Moon belong to the subconscious part of the mind and are passive ones.

The finger mounts

The mounts at the bases of the fingers are also significant in a full analysis of the hand.

The Mount of Jupiter
Situated below the index finger, this indicates ambition and a healthy self-confidence. When it is over-developed, however, it is a sign of arrogance and an excessive desire for prestige. If it is practically flat, it shows an almost total lack of drive and even of self-respect.

The Mount of Saturn
Rising below the middle finger, this is often difficult to see. When it is apparent, though, it indicates a serious temperament. If it is rather large, it can be a sign of a mistrustful, pessimistic outlook.

The Mount of Apollo
Lying below the ring finger, this mount suggests an even and cheerful temperament, as well as some artistic ability. If the mount is very high, then these characteristics may blur into one another and become excessive, taking the form of self-indulgence, affectation and greed, especially for attention. A flat mount, however, indicates a rather dull personality, insensitive to beauty and unmoved by anything that is subtle or that needs perception.

The Mount of Mercury
In its normal form this emphasizes the characteristics which are also indicated by the little finger above it — fluency, swiftness in the use of words, wit. When it is too high, it hints at a tendency to lie and to use trickery; when it is too flat, it points to a dull personality — without humour or quickness of thought, too ready to believe and easily tricked.

Mounts of Mars
Finally, there are the Mounts of Mars. The Upper Mount of Mars, between the Mount of Mercury and the Mount of the Moon, gives an indication of moral courage, although when it is over-developed, it can be a sign of bad temper and a tendency to inflict mental cruelty. Someone whose Upper Mount of Mars is flat is unlikely to stand up for any cause — not even his own. The Lower Mount of Mars, lying between the Mount of Jupiter and the Mount of Venus, suggests self-control and calmness in difficult situations, the sort of cool courage which test pilots or rock-climbers often need. Too big a Lower Mount of Mars may belong to a bully, whereas too flat a mount may be a sign of cowardice.

Mount markings

Often the mounts of the palm and fingers have various shapes on them — crosses, squares, triangles and so on, formed by the fine lines which cover the hand. Of these, the square in particular is thought to be fortunate and to offer protection, while the criss-cross of a grille is thought on the whole to be unfortunate. A triangle is usually taken as a sign that a person has fortune on his side, but when the mount is marked with the cross and the star, the significance of this may depend on where exactly on the mount the marking is located.

Below: the positions of the main lines and mounts. Right: the meanings of the Mount markings.

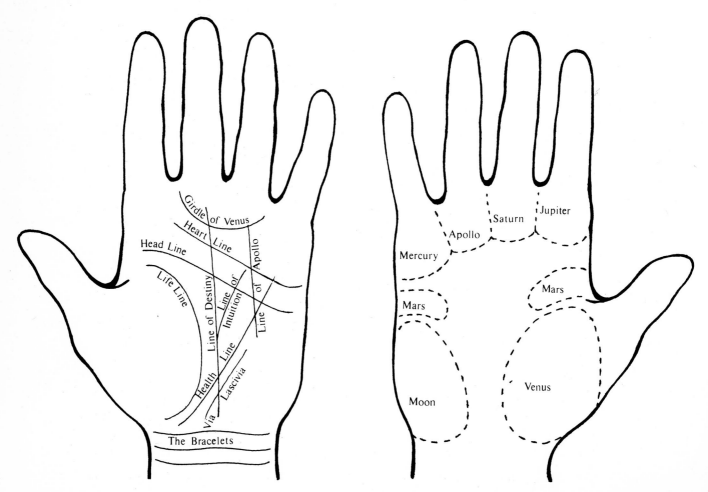

Some of the meanings of these marks are given in the chart below.

The main lines

Having studied the outline and contours of the hand, you will know something about your client, and you can now go on to read the lines of the hand. The three main lines are those of Life, the Head and the Heart. The information they supply will to some extent be modified and added to by the many other lines which cover the palm.

Right versus left hand

In a right-handed person the lines of the left hand indicate the qualities he or she was born with, and those of the right hand the qualities developed and modified by the efforts and accidents of life. In a left-handed person this is, of course, reversed.

Line of life

The Life Line runs from below the Mount of Jupiter and above the Lower Mount of Mars, starting from or bisecting the Head Line, and ending at the heel of the hand, pointing approximately to the middle of the wrist. As its name implies, it gives an indication of physical energy, vitality and strength, but it does not foretell the length of life or the time and nature of death. Nothing read in a palm is certain, partly because the lines themselves alter in varying degrees as time passes.

Life span Because a deep, sharply cut Life Line suggests health, energy and drive, this does indicate the likelihood of a considerable life span. A shorter line is not, in itself, the sign of a short life. It may merely mean a shortage of energy and a need to conserve strength. A line which moves in fits and starts, without being quite broken and with the sections interwoven, indicates variations in levels of energy. A person with such a Life Line will alternate between bursts of energy and periods of fatigue. If the line is really broken, there is a strong possibility that a severe illness or accident has happened at some point.

Ambition Where the Life Line begins has significance, too. If it begins higher than usual, actually on the Mount of Jupiter, it may be a sign of great ambition. Thinner lines cutting the Head Line and reaching up into the Mount of Jupiter also suggest ambition, although ambition probably backed by a sense of proportion.

Calculation If the Life Line begins by forking from the Head Line, the indication is that the energy will be controlled by calculation. The further along the Head Line that this fork occurs, the more control will be exerted. In extreme cases it reaches the point of cunning and results in a complete dependence on calculation, at the life expense of normal feeling and spontaneity. When the line begins below the Head Line, this can be taken as a sign of an impulsiveness that can seem almost uncontrolled at times.

Self-control A chain of lines between Head and Life Lines, before the Life Line breaks away to curve down on its own, suggests a tendency to inward questioning and too much self-control, mixed with periods of excitable, outgoing behaviour.

Line of the head

The Head Line starts halfway between the thumb and index finger, usually right at the edge of the palm, and either runs straight across the palm, stopping anywhere from halfway across to the other edge of the hand, or else curves downward to the Mount of the Moon.

Intelligence There could be some

	Square	Triangle	Star	Grille	Cross
VENUS	Love life without worry	Calculating in love affairs	*Mid-Mount:* sex-appeal; *near wrist:* difficult love life; *near thumb:* long devotion		*One, clearly marked:* a single lifetime love; *many:* a varied love life
MOON	Travel risk-free	Success, fame	Travel risk	Depression and tension	Travel risk
JUPITER	Success	Organizational skill	Unexpected success	Domineering character	Advantageous marriage
SATURN	No money worries	Problem solver	Tragedy threatens	Introspective, undirected	
SUN (APOLLO)	Good name safe	Fame, calmly taken	Influential connections	Vanity, attention-seeker	Disappointment, loss
MERCURY	No tensions	Can influence others, friendly	Success, especially for the studious	Cunning, even dishonest	Beware the dishonesty of others
UPPER MARS	No physical harm			Danger	Danger
LOWER MARS	Danger will not harm	Success in physical combat		Danger	Danger

link between the length and depth of the line and intelligence. It does seem to reflect the type of mind and the way in which this works. A long Head Line may be an indication of a broad and lively understanding. A short Head Line can be a sign of limited intellectual ability, but within the limits there may be intense activity and consequent achievement.

Concentration The depth of the line is what counts here. The deeper and more sharply cut it is, the greater the powers of concentration which it reveals. When the line is chained, this suggests bursts of concentrated mental activity. When it is doubled, with two lines running parallel, it can be a sign of a mind that is disorganized, perhaps to the point of being unbalanced.

Sensitivity A long, straight Head Line suggests a good memory and mental determination. When it slopes down to the Mount of the Moon, it reveals a sensitive temperament, probably in-volved in the arts and certainly creative, but if it continues into the lower part of the Mount, it can be a sign of over-sensitivity, of an inward-looking nature that may suffer from depression.

Caution If the Head Line, as it begins, touches the Life Line, this is an indication of moderation and caution. The longer the two lines remain together, the more pronounced the caution is likely to be, so that decisions will be arrived at slowly and with difficulty.

Irritability If the Head Line crosses the Life Line, having begun on the Lower Mount of Mars, it reveals a tendency to irritability, although a Head Line straight across the hand is a sign that this tendency is at least partly controlled.

Independence Independence and brilliance of mind will show themselves in a slight gap between Head Line and Life Line, but if the Head Line then curves away to the Mount of the Moon, these qualities may be limited by a changeable, over-sensitive temperament. When the space between the two lines is especially wide, there is reason to take this as a sign of reckless-ness, of a tendency to take independence and courage to the point of foolhardiness.

Self-expression A fork at the end of the Head Line suggests skill in self-expression, particularly through the use of words, and the more the line slopes towards the Mount of the Moon, the more marked that skill becomes. A line curving in this way, with a clear fork at the end, indicates literary ability. A three-pronged fork suggests diverse abilities — intelligence, creativity and also good commercial sense. Too large a fork, however, points to too much versatility.

Right versus left hand Check, too, the variation between the line shown on the left hand and that on the right hand. If there is a marked difference,

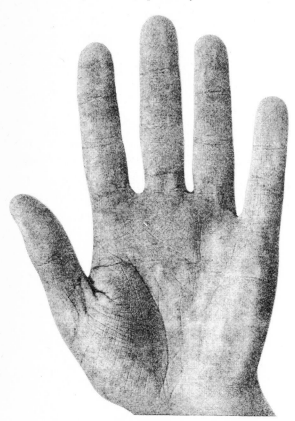
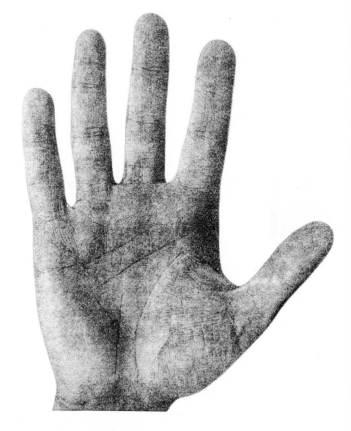

Thom Henvey   Age: 25   Occupation: Writer

Thom has an abundance of energy and strength. The fingers and thumb being fine show a fastidious nature in contrast with his obviously well-developed physique. Only things of quality will interest him for he has a critical eye, but he will be less involved with the material side of life as he gets older and his curiosity about the inner side of things.

His is rather a restless, vacillating nature which does not allow him to sit still for long. He has a lot of ideas, plans and projects which his well developed right hand, giving him energy — shown by the thick base of the hand and heavy finger of Venus — enables him to carry out.

Just about now, an extra Fate line is shown in his hands indicating new responsibilities which he is about to take on himself, but the sound structure of the hands shows that he will cope successfully. It is possible that he is thinking of this new venture right now.

His Head Line is straight, clean cut, long and detached from the Life Line. This indicates success for it shows self-control, speed of thought, attention to detail and a very practical precise execution of work. He is capable of sustained mental effort and can burn the midnight oil with impunity.

His Line of Destiny indicates that at 29 success should be his. After that date Thom can afford to build on the foundation which he has already achieved.

this will show how much basic characteristics have been modified, and even distorted for the sake of making a way in the world.

Line of the heart

The Heart Line rises below the Mount of Mercury and runs across the hand, ending somewhere under or near the Mount of Jupiter. As its name implies, it gives some indication of the depth of feeling of which a person is capable. Its strength, length and depth relate to the profundity and steadiness of the emotions, and its position is important, too. The lower it is on the palm and the more curved the line itself, the more sexuality and sex-appeal will be apparent and the more zest and enjoyment will be shown in love-making. The curve of the line is important, however. If the Heart Line does not rise at the end but finishes a long way below the Mount of Jupiter, this is a sign of reserve and inhibition — an inability to be spontaneous and out-going. If the

line ends by pointing upwards between the fingers of Jupiter and Saturn (the index and middle fingers), take this as showing a great enjoyment of physical pleasure.

Male versus female hands In a male hand, some feminity is indicated by a marked curve downward below the Mount of Jupiter. In a female hand, a similar curve suggests strong masculine elements.

Emotional balance If the line forks on and around the Mount of Jupiter, this has importance, too. A small fork on the Mount of Jupiter points to a steady emotional balance, and to the likelihood of a lasting, harmonious marriage. A wider fork, however, jabbing at the Mount of Saturn as well as the Mount of Jupiter, indicates changeability and self-absorption — a lack of interest in other people. Breaks in the Heart Line may show that there has been an illness of the heart at one time, or an emotional crisis, which probably

ended inconclusively or unhappily.

Romantic predictions

Of course, it is in this connection that people most want to hear prophecies, so here are a few signs to look out for. Little lines branching from the Heart Line indicate romances and affairs — those running upwards being the happy ones, those dropping down from the line the ones which may prove miserable. A chained Heart Line shows at least one affair after marriage.

A break under the finger of Saturn means that a lover has left or will leave. A break under the finger of Apollo shows that it is the person whose hand you are studying who ends the affair.

Overlapping lines point to a quarrel and a break-up, but only a temporary one. A line running from the Heart Line and cutting through the Fate Line points to a marriage which will end unhappily. An island on the line under

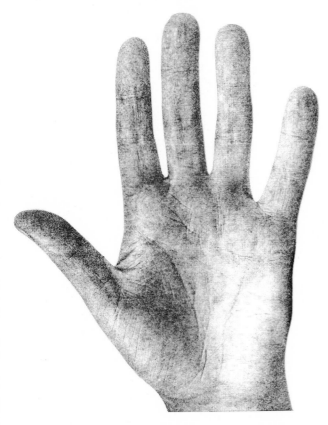 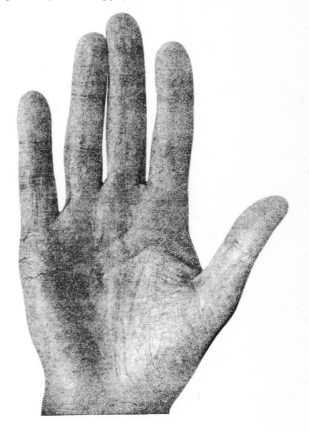

John Fletcher   Age: 29   Occupation: Sales Manager

A great deal of duality exists in his make-up; the conflict is between wanting to go it alone and needing others.

His thumb indicates a very abstract way of looking at life. He likes to ponder things out a good deal. As a youngster, at home, he looked forward to the time when he would be independent. Now he is independent but the finger of Apollo clinging to that of Saturn shows a need for security and a great attachment to the family.

His constitution is not too good and he probably tires easily, but can overcome this by will-power rather than energy potential. This is also borne out by the innate love of fine detail shown in his hand — long Head Line on the left

hand — which is his natural ability; and the desire to delegate such detail — short Head Line on the right hand.

He is very much an individualist and a rebel in his way of expression. His short Head and Heart Lines show he is undemonstrative. He expects to be understood by his actions rather than by his words. This being so, he tends to be misunderstood, but having a good measure of sensitivity (he has fine lines on his hands), he feels this acutely. Consequently his marriage could suffer. Success for John is a matter of harmonizing the dual sides of his nature — shown in the very different appearance of his two hands — and the sharp divergence between his private and public life.

the finger of Saturn suggests an unsatisfactory love affair, one that will bring little happiness. And an island anywhere on the Heart Line points to trouble in love affairs, emotional problems, sexual turmoil, but also to an underlying emotional stability.

Sexual relations The lines which mark sexual relationships run down the edge of the hand, at the side of the Mount of Mercury and between the middle finger. The fainter lines there indicate love affairs, the stronger ones marriages. When they run close to the Heart Line, they show that the affair or the marriage will happen early in life, probably before the age of thirty.

Emotional control Also important is the relation between the Head Line and the Heart Line, for sometimes the temperamental factors that govern these two lines may be in conflict. If the lines lie close together, the emotions are under the control of the mind. If the Heart Line lies very high on the palm, however, this suggests that emotion tends to overrule intelligence and that the subject has a possessive, even a jealous disposition. If a line connects the Head and Heart Lines, it indicates a violent and possibly destructive infatuation. Equally, a line which stretches from the Line of Destiny, the Fate Line, towards the Heart Line without quite reaching it suggests a love affair which will never end in marriage.

Marriage lines The lines indicating marriage also have their own important variations. A break in a marriage line has an obvious meaning, but if the ends overlap, the couple will come together again. If a marriage line curves towards the Heart Line, it is probably that the person whose hand you are looking at will live longer than whoever they marry. If there are tiny downward lines at right angles to a marriage line, your client's marriage-partner may have a long illness. An island on the marriage lines points to infidelity.

Children

Children are indicated by any firm lines which run down to the marriage line from the base of the finger of Mercury — the little finger — and the stronger any of those lines are the greater the likelihood that the child will be a boy.

Girdle of Venus

Sometimes a loosely chained, semi-circular line appears, looping from between the index and middle fingers to between the third and little fingers.

This is known as the Girdle of Venus, for it indicates a deeply passionate nature. The passion need not necessarily show itself sexually, for those with high ideals and an intense involvement in public causes may well have the Girdle on their palms. But it is usually taken as a sign of sexuality. As a result, in the nineteenth century when there was uneasiness about the sexual elements in human make-up, people thought the Girdle of Venus an indication of criminal tendencies and profound instability. Today it can be taken to be no more than a sign of sexual vigour, especially if it is supported by the evidence of a high Mount of Venus. A Girdle broken in the middle shows possible inconstancy, though this would have to be confirmed by other signs in the hand.

Line of Destiny

This line is strongly indicative of the kind of life which a person will live. In terms of character, a well-defined line suggests inner harmony, but a segmented and almost aimless line will be a sign of feelings of inadequacy and an inability to adapt to reality. The place to find the Line of Destiny is near the middle of the hand, running vertically from the wrist towards the middle finger. After adulthood, it changes little, particularly in anyone whose way of life is settled. As a result, the line is much used by palmists making forecasts about their clients' future.

Where it starts Discover where the Line of Destiny starts. If its starting point is almost off the palm, at the first of the lines which run round the wrist, it may belong to someone who has had heavy duties early in life. If it rises from the Life Line, this can be a sign of a cramping early environment, although, if the line continues strongly, this indicates success of life once independence has been achieved. A strong Line of Destiny rising from the Head Line can mean success rather late in life. When it starts from the Mount of Venus, this can show support from a loving family. When the Mount of the Moon is the starting-point, it can mean that help will come from outside the family — and that life will be made exciting but rootless by variety.

Where it ends See how the Line of Destiny ends. If it curves from the Mount of Saturn towards the Mount of Jupiter, you may be looking at the hand of someone who will achieve authority and power over others. If it curves towards the Mount of Apollo, it suggests fame and fortune to come. Any subsidiary line running upward

from the Line of Destiny may be taken as a good sign. Lines that run downward, however, show a likelihood of loss and failure. A Line of Destiny ending at the Head Line suggests eventual failure in life, largely through personal shortcomings and lack of forethought, while one ending at the Heart Line suggests unhappiness in love.

Crosses and linked, chain-like formations If these occur in the Line of Destiny they point to periods of difficulty: a cross at the beginning, for example, suggests a hard childhood, whereas a cross at the end can be a sign that old age will bring difficulties. Breaks in the line are a sign of personal upheavals, but when the fragments overlap, you can assume that the changes which they signify are chosen and not accidental ones.

Line of Apollo

Otherwise known as the Line of the Sun, this runs up from the wrist to the Mount of Apollo. It indicates by its strength good fortune and success. It does not give any clue as to which particular endeavours will bring luck but only indicates that whatever is attempted, good or bad, will have a successful outcome. It overrides by its mere presence many of the negative indications which may exist elsewhere in the palm. If you are reading the hand of someone tempted to become a gambler, a good Line of Apollo might make a sound basis for an otherwise chancy career.

The line should be clear and straight and unflawed. If it is broken or chained, its indications are reversed, for no venture is likely to last long enough to reach success. Naturally, there are few lines which are not flawed in some way, just as there are few lines which are totally successful. If it starts either on the Life Line or the Fate Line, the Line of the Sun indicates high honour and great wealth. When it begins on the Mount of the Moon, however, it tells that this success will be based on approval, amounting to worship, from the opposite sex. Pop stars and film stars are likely to have such a line. If the line rises from the Line of the Head, success will be later in life and will probably be based on intelligence, so the client could be a writer.

Markings on the line A star anywhere along the line of the Sun adds to the amount of luck which the line itself indicates. A series of bars near the beginning of the line shows that early life was hard. When they come later, they indicate the efforts of rivals to discredit your client. A cross, here as elsewhere, is a bad omen and shows that, for a while at least, luck can run out even for the most fortunate people. If the line breaks, look to see how strongly it continues after the break. This indicates no more than a temporary setback if the line is still clearly marked. But there is one sign which overshadows the good fortune shown by the line of Apollo — a deeply hollow palm. A very concave palm always indicates a continuing run of bad luck.

Line of intuition

The line indicating intuitiveness starts just below the little finger. It ends, having traced a shallow, semi-circular course, near the edge of the palm on the Mount of the Moon. If clear, it may be taken to show well-developed psychic powers, and a strong interest in the mystical and the supernatural. See

if the lines on the two palms differ. Someone who has the line deeply engraved on the right hand has worked at these intuitive gifts and developed them consciously. If the lines appear only, or in a much more developed form, on the left hand, intuition is rarely consciously resorted to, but operates subconsciously, prompting decisions which may later be rationalized.

Bracelets

These are the three lines running across the wrist that, if they are clear and distinct, indicate good health and a fortunate and peaceful future. If faint, they signify the opposite of this and if the one nearest the hand is chained, this suggests that a life full of struggle will be crowned by success. Marks in that top bracelet have their significance, too. A star there tells you

that a legacy may be expected. An angle, like a tick beside a correct sum, means something similar — money and honour — but not until after middle age, while a cross indicates a happy old age after a lifetime's struggle.

The lines which begin in the top bracelet are also important. The one leading to the Mount of Apollo indicates a journey to the tropics, while that to the Mount of Mercury predicts unexpected wealth. Look for lines reaching up to the Mount of the Moon, for every one of them indicates that a journey will be taken.

Minor lines

There are a number of other lines, which are by no means invariably present in the palm. This does not matter, since their meaning will not affect a general interpretation.

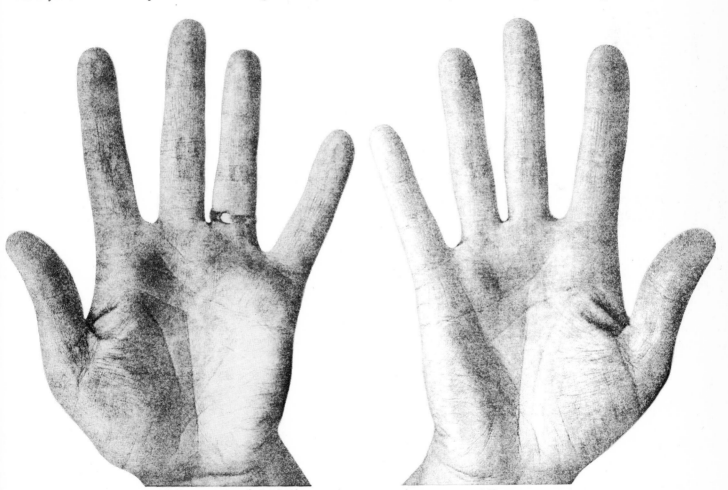

Nicky Hayden   Age: 28   Occupation: Housewife

An impulsive, down to earth, and uncomplicated make-up is shown in the short, straight-set fingers and square palm. Although she is very independent, she is also warm and instinctive. She could have married early, say at eighteen or nineteen years of age. And her strong Heart Line, taken together with the lines for children, seem to indicate a happy, meaningful relationship with probably three children — two boys and a girl.

She has a strong analytical ability — shown in her long finger

of Mercury — and should be good at working with figures as this would use her selective capacities to the full. She can discriminate and sort out what is relevant to the work on hand.

She can expect a change for the better at 28 as her Line of Destiny turns then to the left, and this will make her career more satisfying. And as she gets older she appears to develop the intuitive powers shown in her hand by the strong Line of Intuition.

Fortune in the cards

All playing cards are mysterious. Their curly-bearded kings stare up at us enigmatically, cryptic smiles on their faces. The familiar spades, diamonds, hearts and clubs are potent symbols with many hidden meanings. But what was their beginning? One tradition has it that they were invented by a concubine of the Chinese Emperor S'eun-Ho in 1120 AD. Another indicates that cards may have been used for divination in China two centuries earlier, having possibly come to China from India, crossing the Himalayas to enrich Chinese culture as Buddhism and Yoga had also done. In ancient India, cards were certainly used for augury, the packs being divided into ten suits — one for each incarnation of the Hindu god, Vishnu.

From the start, however, cards seem to have been used as oracles to help resolve people's personal problems. This function almost certainly preceded their association with play and gambling. Most of the skills of early civilizations had a religious aspect, and divination, as the word implies, involves the intervention of the gods.

Some of the European names for cards have derived from Middle Eastern words connected with prediction. The Hebrew word *naibi*, meaning sorcery, and the Arabic *nabi*, meaning to foretell, have given their name to an old Italian card game *naïb*, from which comes the Spanish word for cards, *naipes*. Indeed the Middle East provides another contender to the claim of having invented cards — the ancient Egyptian magician, Hermes Trismegistus. Whether he actually existed, or whether the stories surrounding him are mythical, is not certain, but there remains the possibility that it was under the Pharaohs of the Nile that cards were first employed in the endeavour to throw a little light on human destiny. This theory seemed to make sense when it was believed that the Gypsies originated in Ancient Egypt, for it was certainly the gypsies who spread the use of cards across Europe. But it is now known that the Gypsies first came from India, and so perhaps they brought cards with them from there, over two thousand years ago. Whatever may be the truth of their earliest origins, by the late Middle Ages cards were widespread throughout Europe. And there was a ready audience eagerly seeking their hidden messages—and has been ever since.

The pack

It was probably for the sake of convenience that the seventy-eight cards of the full pack were in the course of time reduced to the familiar fifty-two which we use today. For the art of foretelling the future by cards, known as cartomancy, it is usual to reduce the number to thirty-two. From the full pack, therefore, take the thirty-two cards which have a value of seven or higher, the ace counting as high.

What the individual cards mean

Each card has a meaning, and if you are going to be convincing it will be as well to familiarize yourself thoroughly with these.

It is necessary to remember, however, that certain combinations of cards have a meaning of their own, some of which are given later on. And any card may have its meaning altered by those which lie alongside it.

Since for centuries cartomancy has been mainly an oral tradition, there is bound to be a certain lack of precision, and there is some confusion about the exact meaning of a few of the cards. The most generally agreed meanings of what each of them stands for are given below.

Hearts
Ace Love, warmth, romantic and/or domestic happiness. Good news.
King A generous, handsome man, fair-complexioned.
Queen King's female counterpart, golden-haired and loving.
Jack Friend or lover — but perhaps not always to be trusted.
Ten Success. Good fortune — perhaps unexpected. Happiness.
Nine Fulfilment of hopes. A happy outcome.
Eight Invitation. Perhaps a journey or a visit. Often domestic contentment.
Seven Contentment, especially in marriage.

Spades
Ace Legal matters. A proposition in love or business.
King Lawyer — perhaps a little shady.
Queen Widow or divorcee, subtle and cunning.
Jack A dark, devious, even treacherous, young man.
Ten Worry, begun by a letter. Perhaps a journey — or even imprisonment.
Nine Failure and misfortune.
Eight Sorrow, usually caused by the receipt of bad news.
Seven Quarrels, turbulence — and the receipt of boring advice.

Diamonds
Ace Important letter — and/or ring.
King A man of power and strength.
Queen A gossip. Good-looking, but spiteful.
Jack A messenger, or a man in uniform.
Ten A change, probably a journey.
Nine News, probably concerning money and associated with some new enterprise.
Eight A short, happy journey. (In summer, perhaps a picnic.)
Seven An unexpected gift, or alternatively, hurtful criticism.

Clubs
Ace Success, particularly financial.
King A dark man, friendly and helpful.
Queen Warm, dark woman, affectionate and helpful. Perhaps a widow.
Jack A dark young man, sincere in love.
Ten Sudden money, as in an unexpected legacy.
Nine Financially good marriage.
Eight A dark girl or woman, who brings joy and good fortune.
Seven A small child, perhaps associated with money.

Meaning of suits

Sometimes, when you are laying out the cards, one suit figures more prominently than the others. When this happens, that suit's predominant influence to some extent alters the significance of the other cards. This means that they must be read in the light of that influence. Consequently, it is necessary to know what general feeling is conveyed by each suit.

Hearts
Love, affection, friendship, family and marriage. The emotions, particularly

the warmer, more positive ones. Court cards correspond to people with blond or auburn hair.

Spades
Misfortune and warnings of misfortune. Enemies, scandal and betrayal, suffering and loss. Court cards correspond to people with dark hair.

Diamonds
World affairs, but rarely touching the

extremes of either circumstance or emotion. Court cards correspond to people with blond or auburn hair.

Clubs
Information mainly about friendship, loyalty and money. Thus also worry, anxiety and betrayal. Court cards correspond to brown-haired people.

Client card
The corespondence of court cards to

particular complexions and hair-colourings makes a basis for the selection of one card to represent the person whose fortune you are telling. This card is known as the 'client card'. A fair-haired young woman will be represented by the Queen of Hearts, a fair-haired young man by the King.

An elderly woman with fair, red or grey hair will be represented by the Queen of Diamonds, and a man of similar type by the King.

Dark-haired young men and women are represented respectively by the King and Queen of Clubs.

Dark-haired elderly men and women are represented by the King and Queen of Spades.

The meaning of the other cards can then be related to the way they lie in juxtaposition to the client card.

Here are some examples of the way this works. If your subject is a man and his client card lies next to the Queen of his own suit, this suggests that he will marry soon. If the Queen of Hearts lies next to it, his love will be true, deep and long-lasting. If the Queen of Spades, it suggests a furtive and perhaps guilty affair. If the Queen of Clubs, that he will form a relationship, perhaps a deep friendship, with a wealthy woman.

The Jack of Diamonds next to his client card points to a secret love affair; the Jack of Clubs to money troubles; the Jack of Hearts to some unfaithfulness, and the Jack of Spades to the threat of dishonesty by work colleagues, particularly subordinates. If your subject is a woman, marriage is indicated when her client card lies beside a King of the same colour. A King of the opposite colour suggests a secret love affair. The Jack of Hearts points to a flirtation. The Jack of Diamonds indicates a short-lived infatuation, and the Jack of Spades means an unhappy involvement with a predatory male. If Jacks keep appearing in her cards, the indications are that she may be somewhat indiscriminate in distributing her favours. Whether you mention this will depend on your sense of honesty.

Interconnected meanings

Certain other juxtapositions of cards have an especial significance. The Ten of Diamonds near the client card points to a journey. Near to the Ten of another suit, it suggests a legacy. Near to the Ace of Diamonds, it means a letter, probably from abroad. The Ace of Diamonds itself, when next to the Nine of Spades, indicates a threatened illness. And when next to the Seven of Diamonds, an impending quarrel of some violence. The Ace of Spades near both the Eight and Nine of Spades gives a gloomy reading, suggesting that the future will be heavy with disappointments — friends will betray, business will falter or even fail, deals and arrangements will threaten to collapse.

The Eight of Diamonds raises promises of travel — near any Heart the journey will be short, but near any Club it will be prolonged. If the Seven of Diamonds lies near any Club, the indications are that money will cause problems. A Nine of Diamonds near the client card suggests a path strewn with obstacles. While if the client card is near the Nine of Spades — traditionally a sinister card — there will be bad news and the possibility of illness.

Pairs, triplets, quartets

It is of particular significance when cards of the same value are laid down in pairs, threes, or — most powerfully — fours. These should be looked for first, since the message given by the cards as a whole will be influenced by their meanings.

These meanings have been subject to traditional variations, but the following are the ones most favoured:

Aces
Two Forthcoming marriage.
Three Minor love affair, or flirtation. According to some, excessive credulity.
Four Success.

Kings
Two The portents are good.
Three Considerable success, especially commercial.
Four Great success in all endeavours.

Queens
Two Friendship, but gossip threatens.
Three A visit, but there is jealousy and back-biting.
Four Menace of scandal and slander.

Jacks
Two Bickering will break out.
Three Disharmony, especially within the family. According to some, laziness.
Four Vicious and upsetting quarrels. According to some, success.

Tens
Two Receipt of an unexpected, but probably small, sum of money.
Three Financial and/or legal problems.
Four Good fortune, particularly perhaps in a career.

Nines
Two Limited success, particularly financial. According to some, obstacles.
Three Success. According to some, boredom.
Four A fortunate surprise.

Eights
Two Trouble and argument.

Three Family problems.
Four An anxious, frustrating time.

Sevens
Two An old enemy appears — or perhaps a new lover.
Three A baby will be born.
Four Enemies encircle.

Laying out the cards

Now that you have some idea of what to look for in the cards, what are the forms or shapes in which they should be laid out?

Over the years there have probably been hundreds of ways, as seers and experts frequently devise their own variations. But to start with it is best to use a few methods, each simple to follow, which provide clear readings. These readings must always be supplemented by your own intuition. In order to aid this elusive faculty, the readings must be done in an atmosphere of intense concentration, in itself an aid to belief.

It is always a good idea to ask your subject to shuffle the pack before cutting it because this directs his or her attention closely on to the cards and creates a feeling of expectancy.

Cutting the pack

Cutting is traditionally done with the left hand, because the mystic forces which add to the divinatory power of the cards are supposed to flow through the left, or sinister, hand. The subject should certainly always cut the cards, even if he or she does not shuffle them.

Reading your own cards

By and large, it is not advisable to use the following methods of laying out cards for trying to divine your own fortune. Traditionally they are intended to answer the questions of others, using powers and energies for which you are supposed to be the neutral channel.

There are, however, a number of games of patience (solitaire) whose object is to give answers to one's own questions. Usually these work on the basis that if they do not come out, the answer is 'No', and circumstances are not propitious.

The wizard
One method which seems to demand a fair amount of co-operation from Fate is known as the Wizard. You take the thirty-two card pack and begin laying down the cards face upward. As

you lay down the first card, you say out loud "Seven". Then as you lay down the next card you say "Eight", and so on until you have called "Ace", when you start again with "Seven". Whenever you actually lay down a card which corresponds to the value you have called, put it to one side. Keep going through the pack until it is exhausted — or until you are.

The more swiftly you and Fate discard the cards, the better augury it is. If the cards and your calling do not coincide at all, or only at very long intervals, you may assume that your project is, for the time being, unlikely to prove successful.

Reading other people's cards

Some of the methods of laying out cards for divination for a client follow. The one thing that they all have in common is that you need to use your imagination and intuition to interpret the messages they have to offer.

It is for this reason, as well as to foster confidence, that you should learn the meanings of the cards by heart. Only when you have them immediately available will you be able to string them together into coherent and evocative predictions.

Cartomancers have a saying that the cards get tired, and this may be true if they are really under some external influence. Many people believe in the existence of psychic powers, and cartomancy is one way to concentrate them if you have any. But it seems they should never be abused by too much use, or by a shallow approach.

Limit your card readings, therfore, to one session an evening, or at most two, divided by a period of rest. Only do some half-dozen readings at each session. If the other people present want to hear what you see in their cards, let them wait for a future occasion.

Finally, one small warning. People take predictions of this sort more seriously that they themselves may realize. If you find yourself faced with what seems a very gloomy forecast, reflect if a little diplomacy might not be in order. Illness or bankruptcy are serious subjects. And while warnings are not threats, predictions have a way of influencing behaviour, If, therefore, you are faced with a row of cards heavy with Spades, you might be well-advised to make a compromise between honesty and optimism. A little consideration for your friends' peace of mind cannot come amiss.

The fan

For this method, spread the cards face down on the table, and ask the subject to draw thirteen at random.

Take these thirteen cards and spread them face upward, in a fan shape.

Look to see if the client card which represents your subject is there, or the seven of the same suit which may act as its substitute. If neither appears, you can either begin again or take it as an indication that the moment is not propitious for divination.

Taking the client card first, count the cards off in fives, from left to right, reading every fifth card, and always using the card you have just read as the first of the next five. (Naturally you do not read the client card, but continue until you have read all the other twelve.) Next ask the inquirer to pick five more cards from what remains of the pack left face down on the table. Spread these out face upward in a separate fan. These cards are read in pairs. The first and fifth together, then the second and the third. The middle card is read by itself.

Reading

Here is a reading of the cards which appear in the photograph opposite, top. The inquirer is a fair-haired girl, so the client card will be the Queen of Hearts.

First consider the cards as a whole. Clubs predominate — although only slightly. Bear in mind that money may be important in the reading. There is a pair of Sevens, and these might indicate a new lover — or an old enemy — erupting into her life.

Beginning with the client card, and counting off the cards in sets of five, the first card to be read is the Seven of Diamonds, indicating a gift, and this is followed by the treacherous but darkly handsome Jack of Spades. Then the bait of an advantageous marriage is dangled by the Nine of Clubs. The Seven of Hearts indicates contentment in marriage — a trait not normally connected with the Jack of Spades.

The Seven of Clubs gives a child associated with money. This may be involved with a legacy, for it is followed by news about money indicated by the Nine of Diamonds.

From here on, the marriage signs become clearer, for in the Jack of Clubs a new suitor appears, honest and sincere. He is more the type to lead to the contented marriage already indicated and he may well be the lover indicated by the adjacent pair of Sevens.

The Nine of Hearts suggests that hopes will be fulfilled, a suggestion reinforced by the Eight of Hearts with its hint of domestic felicity.

The Ace of Clubs offers financial success, probably by way of the Ace of Spade's new proposition. This could possibly be made by the affectionate, although widowed, Queen of Clubs. (She could be understood to be the new lover's mother.)

All this is confirmed by the first pair of the supplementary five cards, the Ten of Clubs suggesting unexpected money, and the Ace of Diamonds an important letter.

But now there is bad news. The money may have to do with someone's illness, perhaps even the death of someone close because the Ten and the Eight of Spades in juxtaposition make a formidably unpleasant pair. But the King of Diamonds is a man of power, a tower of strength. If your subject trusts in his ability, she will come through this final crisis.

To summarize this information:

First, the client is being pressed to marry a young man whom she does not trust because it would be financially advantageous for both of them to do so. She should resist, for a new and truly loving suitor will appear through whom both happiness and money may be hers. Nevertheless, a crisis is brewing. Someone close to her is likely to be very ill, and an anxious time will follow. She should trust the strong man, friend or relation, who will appear at that time to help her bear the strain.

The seven cards

After your client has shuffled and cut the pack, draw out each seventh card, putting the six cards in between to the bottom of the pack each time.

When you have twelve cards, spread them out from left to right in the order in which you draw them.

Select the client card. If it is not there, take it from the remainder of the pack. If it is there, draw a thirteenth card at random from the pack and lay it with the others.

Beginning with the client card, count off seven cards, reading the last one. Continue in this way, reading every seventh card. When you have read all the cards, shuffle the thirteen cards again, and ask the client to cut them (with the left hand, of course). Spread the top six cards face upwards in a line. On the first five of these, place one additional card, leaving the sixth by itself. Then on the first two, lay down two cards which you have left.

The first little stack of three cards represents the subject as a person. The second stack of three cards stands for the house or apartment he or she lives in. The next stack of two cards shows what is expected to happen. The fourth stack represents what is not expected, the fifth stands for the real surprises that are lying in wait. The final, single, card will tell your subject's thoughts or wishes.

Reading

Opposite (below) is the second stage, the 'seventh cards' having already been drawn. The client is a man, well-set-up, middle-aged (his client card was the King of Clubs), who is married.

Begin with the three cards on the left, which relate to him directly, and they tell us that he made a financially helpful marriage (Nine of Clubs) with a warm, affectionate lady as dark-haired as himself (Queen of Clubs) and that he either likes travel and change or has very recently come back from a significant voyage (Ten of Diamonds).

Next, his house: it is a source of worry, sometimes feels like a prison (Ten of Spades), he has a neighbour who makes him feel uneasy (Jack of Hearts), but his house has accommodation for a child, probably a nursery.

He nevertheless expects, the next column shows, to remain contented in his marriage (Seven of Hearts) and anticipates seeing someone close to him in uniform (Jack of Diamonds).

There are shocks in store, coming by way of an unreliable lawyer (King of Spades) — but the outcome will be unexpectedly happy (Six of Hearts).

A relationship, perhaps a marriage, between two mature friends of his, both with a great capacity for affection (King of Clubs and Queen of Hearts) will be the real surprise the next few weeks will bring.

Then, his wish. Here the Eight of Hearts echoes the Ten of Diamonds in the first column: what he really wants is the chance to travel.

The mystic star

From the thirty-two cards, pick out the client card and lay it up in the middle of the table.

Your client, having shuffled the rest of the pack, cuts it twice, placing the resulting three piles face downward. You then turn each pile the right way up, and read the top cards thus revealed, first one by one, then in combination. This is called a general

indication and will give you an overall idea of the way fortune is running for your subject. The client now reshuffles the pack.

You take the top eight cards and, in an anti-clockwise direction, lay them face downward at regular intervals around the client card, which still remains in the centre of the table. It is in this way that you form the mystic, eight-pointed star.

Your client now takes the rest of the pack, and on each of the eight cards lays two more, working round the circle twice and setting the cards face down one at a time.

One by one, still working anti-clock-wise, turn each little stack of three face upward. Read the information all three cards provide in conjunction.

Reading

The client card, the Queen of Spades, shows that we are considering the fortune of a dark, middle-aged, married lady.

The general indication, which was gleaned from the Nine of Spades, was of changes, with some steep ups and downs likely.

The first column, directly above the client card, certainly suggests a down-turn in fortune: a shady lawyer (King of Spades) and a man of power (King of Diamonds) combine to bring about the client's failure (Nine of Spades). Moving leftward, we discover news (Nine of Diamonds) of a romance (Ace of Hearts) involving a very dear friend, probably blonde (Queen of Hearts). Since she is known for her generosity, it is probably her gift (Seven of Diamonds) which leads to a journey (Ten of Diamonds), almost certainly to visit her and discuss the financially advisable marriage (Nine of Clubs) which is in the offing.

But what of the client's own life? A new proposition (Ace of Spades) leads to an unexpected success (Ten of Hearts), one of the sudden ups in her

fortunes, which in turn gives her the chance of another journey (Eight of Hearts).

Can it be this which leads to domestic quarrels (Seven of Spades)? If so, financial success, already indicated above, now appears again (Ace of Clubs) and married happiness results for her (Seven of Hearts).

Yet now a new worry will appear, which seems to involve her daughter, the dark girl (Eight of Clubs). A letter arrives (Ten of Spades) concerning a dark young man (Jack of Clubs) who loves the girl. Correspondence ensues, for the Ace of Diamonds points to a very important letter — probably from the dark, friendly man (King of Clubs) who appears to be the young man's father. And the King of Hearts, a generous, affectionate friend, takes a hand in the affair. Despite the intervention of the spiteful and gossipy Queen of Diamonds, the arrival of the young man's mother, warm and likeable (Queen of Clubs), leads on to a short, happy and joyful journey (Eight of Diamonds) which one can only suppose will be taken to the sound of wedding bells.

To summarize, despite an initial setback in a legal matter, a new venture will lead to financial success and domestic contentment. A friend will seek advice about a proposed marriage, and the client's own daughter, after a short period of anxiety, will go happily to the altar with the approval of almost everyone concerned.

Single question

There are a number of systems for answering one question at a time. Let the client ask his or her question. There are then several methods of seeing how the cards will answer it.

Four Aces

One involves the four Aces. After your client has shuffled the thirty-two card pack, lay the top thirteen cards face up on the table, putting aside any Aces. Gather up all the cards again, having shuffled them as before, lay out another thirteen from the top, and again pick out any Aces. Repeat this a third time. Be careful to keep the Aces in the order in which they have appeared. The sooner the Aces do appear, the better for your client. The order in which they appear is very significant, the early cards having greater power than the later.

Thus the Ace of Spades, if picked out first, overshadows the other three, meaning nothing will be achieved without difficulty.

First seven cards

An even shorter method of answering a particular question consists of laying the first seven cards of the pack face down in a row, then turning up the first, fourth and seventh cards. These will provide the information you need for your answer. But here, of course, you need to remember the meanings of individual cards, as well as the significance of each suit.

Sometimes, of course, the answers given by the cards seem to make no sense at all. If this happens, you must remember that the information they are offering has to do with the future, in which there may well be other factors involved which will give the cards an unexpected relevance. So it is always a good idea to note down which cards have appeared, for they may yet become important.

However, if they do seem to be jumbled and meaningless, it is permissible to lay them down a second time, but no more. If on the second occasion too they reveal nothing, that must in itself be taken as a message. Like any other oracle, the cards reserve the right to keep their silence.

Reading

The commonest single question, of course, concerns love and its ramifications.

With the layout below a young lady asked the plainest question of all: 'Does he love me?' The Ace of Hearts, telling of warmth, domestic happiness and affection, seems to give the answer she is hoping for. But who is the dark lady, helpful and friendly, for which the Queen of Clubs must stand? 'Oh, his mother — she likes me', the girl says, at once. The Seven of Diamonds stands for an unexpected gift. In this context, almost certainly an indication that the young man will himself, quite suddenly and quite soon, indicate how he feels.

The weekly forecast

For this it is not necessary to learn the individual meanings of cards. All that is needed is an awareness of what the four suits as a whole represent.

Ask your subject to shuffle and then cut the pack into three piles. Take the top card of each pile, and lay it face down on the table in front of you. Begin with the left-hand pile, and end with the right.

Take the remaining cards in the three piles, ask the client to shuffle and cut as before, and once again place the top card from each pile face down on the table. These should be placed alongside the original three, so that there is now a row of six.

Repeat this operation three times more, so that you end up with a row of fifteen cards.

Turn over the two cards at either end of the row. These will give you the general fortune for the following day, determined by the symbols and colours revealed. The right-hand card relates to the morning, the left-hand card to later in the day. (If you had Spades on the right and Hearts on the left, it might suggest early disaster, followed by affection or comfort later on.)

Working inwards, two by two, gradually turn up fourteen cards. These will give you the seven day sequence of the week's fortune. The points value of each card may be important, for if the suit is unlucky, as Spades tend to be, the numbers revealed should be avoided on the day in question. Equally, numbers in a lucky suit should be followed up.

This leaves the central, fifteenth card still face down on the table. Use it to answer a question — the suit of the card will give you the reply. If your subject is anxious about some action to be taken in a love affair, a Heart would be an encouraging card to turn up. While for someone with a business query a Club would be preferable. For all questions, a Spade suggests that postponement of any plans might be the safest course.

Reading

A forecast of this kind was done every Sunday for the manager of a small factory. In this instance the Diamonds show for the next two mornings that conditions for business during these first days of the week remain equable. The evenings, meanwhile, display Hearts, which suggests that affection, perhaps love, will flower then.

The third day, Wednesday, has Clubs all day: a worrying day with some money problems seems likely. The next morning, Clubs persist — perhaps there is also a question of loyalty to a friend and a colleague, probably a woman, which must be decided. By the afternoon, however, the King of Hearts indicates that their friendship is restored. Saturday morning is a good time, with Diamonds back on display, to catch up on work lost during the midweek crisis; the afternoon, however, produces more problems, perhaps at home or with a neighbour. This is, if anything, intensified on Sunday morning when there is scandal in the offing, double-dealing, possibly domestic strife. By the afternoon, however, things seem on an even keel once more, and the client can relax and prepare to start work the following week.

The central card remains, answer to a single important question. On this occasion the man asked whether he should employ a particular young man. Clubs indicate steadfastness and loyalty, so the answer here is affirmative: the man should be taken on.

Temple of fortune

This more elaborate method was invented by a famous cartomancer in pre-Revolution Paris, when the glories of the mid-eighteenth century were collapsing in the uncertainty which preceded the storming of the Bastille. Ask the client to shuffle and cut the pack as usual, then lay it out, each card face upward, in the following manner.

Starting at the bottom of the column, lay six cards sideways, one above the other, on the right-hand side of the table. Similarly, lay six cards sideways, one above the other and starting at the bottom, on the left-hand side of the table.

Now place four cards sideways, again starting from the bottom, immediately to the left of the first column, in such a way that these four cards are opposite the spaces between the lower five cards of the column.

Now place five cards in the upright position, from right to left, in a row which is level with the top card of the right-hand column, thus making a connecting row with the top card of the left-hand column.

Now lay down another four cards, sideways again and working from the top, immediately to the right of the left-hand column, so that they lie opposite the spaces between the lower five cards of the right-hand column.

Finally, above the connecting row of upright cards, lay another upright row consisting of the last seven cards of the pack.

The two rows of sideways cards on the right reveal the past. The two rows of sideways cards on the left reveal the future. And the two rows of upright cards are concerned with the present. The three outer rows of cards give the primary indications in each case. The inner rows modify what the outer rows tell you. The order of the cards is, as always, of some significance. They should be read in the order in which you laid them down.

Below: The arrangement of cards which gives the weekly forecast discussed in the text. Above right: A temple of fortune — one of the more elaborate ways of reading the cards which is described in detail here.

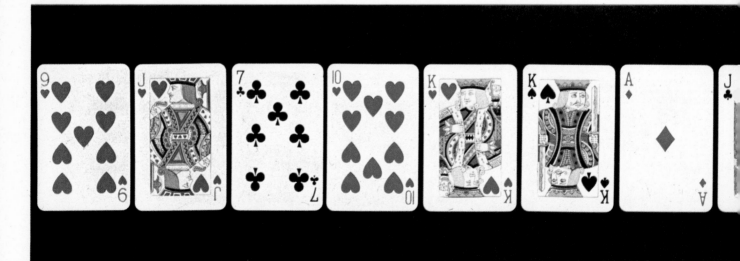

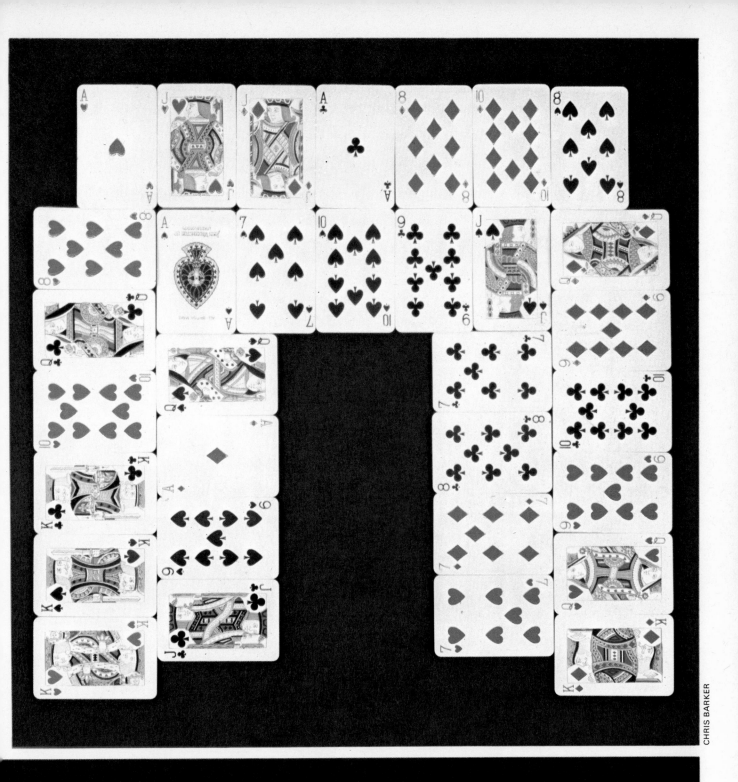

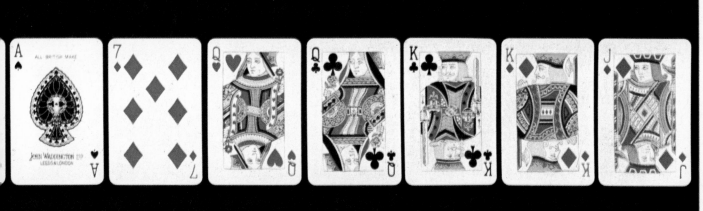

The mysterious Tarot pack

LE MAT.

LE BATELEUR

L'AMOUREUX.

LE CHARIOT

LA JUSTICE

L'ERMITE

TEMPERANCE

LE DIABLE.

LA MAISON DE DIEU

L'ÉTOILE

JUNON.

L'IMPERATRICE

L'EMPEREUR

JUPITER.

LA ROUE DE FORTUNE

LA FORCE

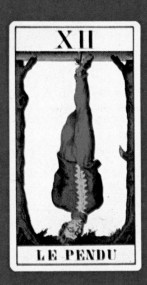

LE PENDU

LA MORT.

LA LUNE

LE SOLEIL

LE JUGEMENT

LE MONDE

Most people regard Tarot cards with a degree of awe. Their age-old designs and symbols, their haunting figures, are deeply rooted in myths which remain mysteriously just beyond the boundaries of certain knowledge. It is easy to believe what these cards tell us and, involuntarily, to handle them with a feeling of solemnity, a sense of taking part in a very ancient ritual. Curious, and sometimes anxious, people have for many centuries consulted the Tarot. Partly because of their long history, and partly because of the power with which history has invested them, the Tarot cards are accepted by many people to whom no other system of fortune-telling makes the slightest appeal. It is, in a sense, the aristocrat of oracles.

Origins of Tarot

No one knows where these mysterious and potent cards were first devised. They have, however, consistently been linked with the Gypsies, who have long been regarded as the guardians of a secret branch of knowledge. This knowledge may have come from religious mysteries of pagan Greece, or the divine lore of the Chaldeans. What is true, is that both Tarot and Gypsies seem to have appeared in Europe during the period between the eleventh and fourteenth centuries.

Jacques Gringonneur, a fourteenth-century astrologer, sometimes credited with the invention of playing cards, almost certainly based the pack he devised for Charles VI of France on the Tarot.

The modern Tarot pack is based on the researches of an eighteenth-century French scholar named de Gebelin. His book *Le Monde Primitif* contained illustrations of the cards. It is this 'Marseilles pack' from which almost all the other Tarot packs used in the West have been derived.

The position of the Joker in the sequence has caused a certain amount of controversy. Many authorities have written works on the significance of the cards. But, untroubled by these discussions and differencies, Gypsies and others have used them to read the characters and fortunes of the thousands of people who have come to consult them.

Each pack of Tarot cards comes with instructions and interpretations. These are sometimes somewhat briefly or quaintly expressed, so below there is a simple explanation of the meanings of the cards.

Some people maintain that you should memorize all these meanings but you can, of course, refer back to the written word. And sceptics may be more inclined to believe your predictions if they see you referring to a text and interpreting it rather than apparently making the whole thing up as you go along! Belief depends a great deal on atmosphere.

The Major Arcana

The twenty-two cards of the Major Arcana, the Trumps, are subtle and complex symbols. They have a relation with the twenty-two letters of the Hebrew alphabet and the twenty-two branches of the Tree of Life which has a very prominent place in the Kabbala.

The Fool
Appearing anywhere, this card alters the meaning of the others. It is the free force in life, for it offers the inquirer a choice between good and evil, wisdom and folly.
Reversed: The choice may be bad and thoughtless.

1. Magician
Organization, control over natural forces, hence willpower. Suggests creative, perhaps artistic, ability.
Reversed: Weakness, force used destructively.

2. Priestess
The unseen, reached by divinatory power, thus an indication of unseen influences at work. Intuitive ability.
Reversed: Self-love, vanity, sensuality, superficiality.

3. Empress
The Earth Mother, thus fertility and marriage, wealth, the proper material rewards of endeavour.
Reversed: Barrenness, endeavour thwarted, resources dwindled.

4. Emperor
Determination, leadership, authority. The aid of powerful allies. A strong but well-controlled and directed sexuality.
Reversed: Immaturity, lack of control, subservience.

5. High Priest
Otherwise called the Hierophant or Pope. Stands for formal subjects: theology, ritual, law. Thus, acceptance of the conventions and hence social and material success.
Reversed: Inventiveness.

6. The Lovers
Harmony, balance between inner and outer, sacred and profane. Thus choice, based on attraction, hence success in love and — probably — marriage.
Reversed: Disharmony, unfaithfulness quarrels, perhaps divorce.

7. The Chariot
Triumph over financial difficulties, rivals and above all, over illness. Thus an indication of success in many areas.
Reversed: Ill health, undeserved success, restlessness.

8. Justice
Balance, legality, pedantry. Accountability for one's actions.
Reversed: Inequality, injustice. Merciful attitude to others.

9. Hermit
Meditation, prudence, receiving higher guidance. Thus a meeting with a wise counsellor who should be heeded.
Reversed: Immaturity, refusal to accept good advice.

10. Wheel of Fortune
Change, alteration — the endless highs and lows of life. Thus, unexpected change of fortune, sudden success.
Reversed: Failure and setbacks, demanding perseverance.

11. Strength
Courage, force of character, spiritual power triumphant over carnality. Thus the ability to overcome adversity, and hence any ill fortune shown in adjacent cards is modified.
Reversed: Materialism, lack of moral strength.

12. Hanged Man
To the spiritual — spiritual advancement. To the unaware — possible ill fortune. A pause in life, a withdrawal to develop inwardly. Thus, intuition, spirituality.
Reversed: Egotism, arrogance, false spirituality.

13. Death
Change, an ending — followed by a new beginning, perhaps in consciousness. Calm after a storm, reward after travail. But also, self-destructive fear.
Reversed: Inertia, stagnation. Revolution, perhaps assassination.

14. Temperance
Harmony with others, adaptation, successful timing.
Reversed: Quarrels, conflict of interests, separation.

15. Devil
Temptation, choice. Sometimes could

be inhumanity, carnality, illness.
Reversed: Dawn of spirituality and humility. Indecision.

16. Tower

Also known as the House of God. Catastrophe, undeserved disaster. Life style and ideas upset, permitting new enlightenment, but present material ambitions are likely to be thwarted.
Reversed: Oppression, perhaps false imprisonment. But through misfortune, freedom of body or spirit is gained.

17. Star

Hope, inspiration. Happiness-possibly fleeting. Spirituality glimpsed. Good health.
Reversed: Pessimism, obstinacy, gloom. Ill health.

18. Moon

Deception, secret enemies, unforeseen danger. Love misdirected or a loved one threatened. Intuitive powers increased.
Reversed: Practicality, avoidance of risk — but peace after storm.

19. Sun

Ambitions attained, material success, happy marriage, contentment — though none of these without proper labour.
Reversed: Plans unsettled. Loss, perhaps of job. Marriage problems.

20. Judgement

Awakening, new awareness. Strong

influence of Fate. Spiritual union with the Absolute is near.
Reversed: Separation, disillusionment, loss of worldly goods.

21. World

Reward, success, fulfilment — not always in the way expected. State of cosmic consciousness and spiritual liberation.
Reversed: Fear of change, cramping of vision, success elusive.

The Minor Arcana

There are fifty-six cards in the Minor Arcana. They are divided into four suits: Cups, Swords, Pentacles and Wands (or Rods). These are the equivalents of Hearts, Spades. Diamonds and Clubs. There are fifty-six because each suit has an extra card, having four court cards instead of three: King, Queen, Knight and Knave.

The meanings of the suits

It is useful to remember that the suits have a significance of their own, and that a preponderance of one over the others slants the whole interpretation.
Cups Love, generosity, goodness.
Swords Disagreement, quarrels, strife.
Pentacles Intrigue. plots, politics.
Wands Change, travel, opportunity.
Upright or reversed, each of these fifty-six cards has a divinatory meaning and can alter the information which

the Tarot pack gives us. But the main significance always lies in the Major Arcana and in the evocative and almost frightening power of the figures it portrays. The Minor Arcana can do no more than modify the broad outlines of the analyses and forecasts these stronger figures give. It tells of people's abilities and manoeuvres while they are protected or threatened by the greater forces which the Major Arcana represents.
Of course, anyone who wants to practice Taromancy seriously will have to learn the significance of, say, the Six of Pentacles as carefully as that of the High Priest or the Chariot, for its evidence may prove vital in the end.

The appeal of Tarot

It is clear that the Tarot pack can reach down to deep levels of the subconscious mind. Some people, when they see you produce a deck of these cards and proceed to lay them out, will, despite themselves, feel the tiny shiver of apprehension, of delight mixed with fear, which most of us experience when faced by the unknown, the uncanny, or the supernatural.
If you have learned to master the complexities of reading the Tarot pack, you have one certain way of stirring people's curiosity and holding their interest which you will have undoubtedly earned. For, besides knowing the meanings of each of the seventy-eight

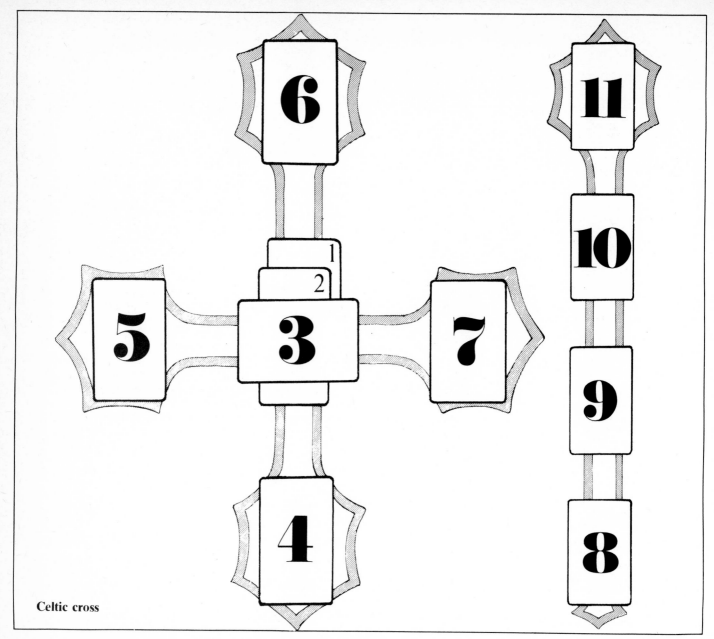

Celtic cross

cards, the reading calls for a high level of intuition, plus the intelligence to combine the individual meanings with the promptings of intuition into one coherent interpretation. If you do achieve this mastery, there is no question that you and your friends will have a new pastime — and perhaps something more.

Lay-out of the Tarot cards

First, as in simple Cartomancy, choose a 'client' card. How, or even whether, you use it, will vary from one lay-out to another. The subject should then shuffle the cards. If you do it yourself, it helps if, before cutting the pack, the client lays a hand on it. Ask the client to concentrate on the questions to be asked.

Using the left hand, the client then cuts the pack into three piles, setting each pile down to the left of the one

before. Pick up the first of the piles laid down, also with your left hand, and begin laying out the cards in the pattern you have chosen. There are dozens of these, as one might expect after so many centuries of practice. Here are two of the most common:

Celtic cross

Place the 'client' card in the centre of the table. Now, in sequence and face up, lay out ten cards as follows:

Covering Card placed over the 'client' card. This gives the influence at work around the client in question.

Crossing Card laid sideways across the 'client' and Covering cards (though read as if upright). This shows what the opposing forces are. Note that if the Covering card is unfavourable, these opposing forces may be good.

Beneath Laid directly below the central cards, to form the first arm of a cross. This points to a past experience

relevant to the matter in hand.

Behind Laid to the left of the central cards, to form the second arm of the cross. This shows an influence just passing.

Crowning The upper arm of the cross — a possible future event.

Before The right-hand arm of the cross. This points to events in the very near future.

Now to the right of the cross, four cards are laid in a vertical row, starting from the bottom:

Fears The bottom card. This reveals the outcome of which the client is most afraid.

Environment Second from bottom. This card sums up the opinions of family and friends on the matter.

Hopes What does the client hope will happen?

Outcome The top card, and the last. This includes in summary the message of all the other cards, as well as

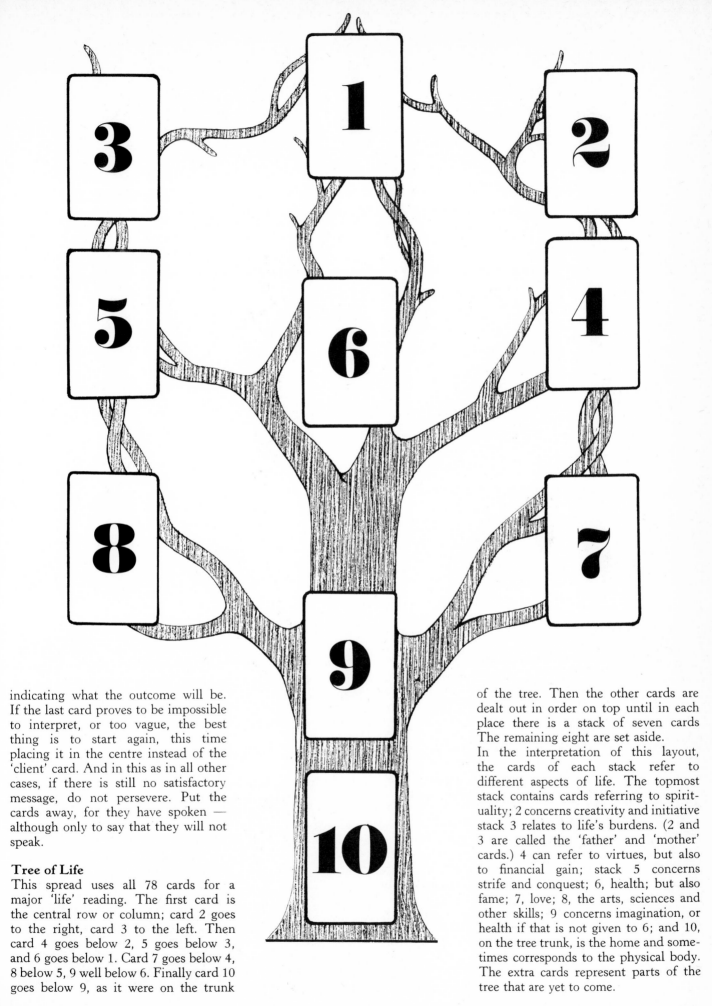

indicating what the outcome will be. If the last card proves to be impossible to interpret, or too vague, the best thing is to start again, this time placing it in the centre instead of the 'client' card. And in this as in all other cases, if there is still no satisfactory message, do not persevere. Put the cards away, for they have spoken — although only to say that they will not speak.

Tree of Life

This spread uses all 78 cards for a major 'life' reading. The first card is the central row or column; card 2 goes to the right, card 3 to the left. Then card 4 goes below 2, 5 goes below 3, and 6 goes below 1. Card 7 goes below 4, 8 below 5, 9 well below 6. Finally card 10 goes below 9, as it were on the trunk

of the tree. Then the other cards are dealt out in order on top until in each place there is a stack of seven cards The remaining eight are set aside.

In the interpretation of this layout, the cards of each stack refer to different aspects of life. The topmost stack contains cards referring to spirituality; 2 concerns creativity and initiative stack 3 relates to life's burdens. (2 and 3 are called the 'father' and 'mother' cards.) 4 can refer to virtues, but also to financial gain; stack 5 concerns strife and conquest; 6, health; but also fame; 7, love; 8, the arts, sciences and other skills; 9 concerns imagination, or health if that is not given to 6; and 10, on the tree trunk, is the home and sometimes corresponds to the physical body. The extra cards represent parts of the tree that are yet to come.

The ancient I Ching

The Book of Changes, which is I Ching in Chinese, is very old. Confucius and Lao Tse, founders of the two great streams of Chinese philosophy, turned to it for inspiration and information. It was regarded with such awe that in 213 BC, when the Emperor Ch'in Shih Huang Ti ordered a wholesale burning of books, it was one of the few which escaped. Its poetic teachings and symbolic commands, rich in metaphor, have had a great influence on the literature of China. Its intriguingly imprecise prophecies about the future were, until very recently, constantly referred to by the Chinese people, and those experienced in the interpretation of the I Ching were to be found in every village, almost in every street.

The philosophy

It is hard to say whether the I Ching reflected an already existing body of Chinese thought, or whether Chinese philosophy has been influenced by it to such an extent that it has almost derived from it. Certainly it is concerned with the duality of Yin and Yang, which is, very roughly, the opposition of the male — Yin — and the female — Yang — principles. Yin and Yang also stands for the tension between light and dark, the firm and the yielding, the sky and the earth. What is important for consideration of the Book of Changes is that such a state of universal tension means that the world is not static or inert. The ancient Chinese thinkers always rejected the notion of a motionless universe. They considered that events on this earth only mirrored the real events, which occured in a very different sphere, out of reach of all but a handful of the most highly developed human beings. So, what the I Ching offers is information about a world in flux — as its name implies, it is concerned with changes, with the driving forces which constantly modify life. Since the book is concerned with action, rather than with a static picture of an unalterable state, it is also concerned with morality, with ideas of right and wrong. These are dealt with in the Judgements which accompany the pre-

The traditional Chinese way to cast hexagrams was with yarrow sticks.

dictions. They give the I Ching a dimension which no other method of scanning the future has. It not only predicts courses of action, it also gives some indication of whether their outcome will be beneficial or harmful. Consequently, people who consult the I Ching have an element of choice in their actions.

The role of fate

Underlying the morality of the I Ching is a belief in the prime importance of Fate. Changes happen all the time and everywhere, and this perpetual dynamic process depends upon the operation of Fate. The Chinese believed that God and Creation must get their energy from the workings of Fate. But these workings may be influenced and changed if anyone can put himself, as it were, in the place of a god and survey the future. The oracle in the I Ching allows that to be done. It does so by using the totality of every event, by treating nothing that occurs as being without meaning. Fate, or the mysterious supernatural forces through which it works, are everywhere and unceasingly active. The problem is to understand what their activity means.

Using the I Ching

First you need the book itself. This is freely available both in hardback and in paperback editions. Next you need either three coins or yarrow sticks. The latter are available from Chinese or fortune-telling shops. (Or you could, of course, find them growing wild and dry them yourself.) The book gives clear instructions on how to proceed from there — how to toss the coins or select the yarrow sticks, arrive at a hexagram and interpret it — to obtain a full reading.

The hexagrams

Of the two ways in which the I Ching may be consulted the first, using sticks, is rather complex and the other, using coins, is much simpler. Both methods, however, permit you to pick out the particular oracular statement which answers your question. Basically, these statements are an arrangement of six complete or broken lines,

forming a Hexagram.

In time past, it was believed that the oracle worked with the utmost simplicity, so that a complete line meant 'Yes', a broken one 'No'. But this came to seem inadequate, and the unbroken and the broken lines were joined in four combinations, and a third line was added to them. This gave the possibility of eight arrangements, or trigrams, to each of which a particular meaning was given. These symbols were again combined, and the arrangements changed from three to six lines. This achieved two results: each symbol became far richer in meaning, and the number of symbols was at once increased from eight to sixty-four. The I Ching had, in its essence, been created.

Method of consultation

The hexagram which answers a particular question is built up line by line.

The yarrow sticks
The Chinese sages used yarrow sticks and a complicated formula to arrive at the hexagram they wanted. This is described in detail in the book.

Coins
The alternative method, using coins, is much more practical today. In ancient times, the Chinese themselves used brass coins with a hollow in the middle, but ordinary coins will do as well. Three of these are used, with heads being given the value of three, tails that of two.

The three coins are tossed and the value they make together, once they come to rest, will be six, seven, eight or nine. The first two stand for broken lines, the last two for unbroken lines. Thus, each throw of the coins gives a line of one sort or the other and when you have thrown six times, you will have the hexagram you need. In the key with which each copy of the Book of Changes is provided you now look up the hexagram's number, and in this way find the page which tells you its meaning.

Interpretation

At this point, however, things become both more complicated and more interesting.

	Name	Attribute	Image	Family Relationship
☰	Chi'en the Creative	strong	heaven	father
☷	K'un the Receptive	devoted, yielding	earth	mother
☳	Chên the Arousing	inciting movement	thunder	first son
☵	K'an the Abysmal	dangerous	water	second son
☶	Kên Keeping Still	resting	mountain	third son
☴	Sun the Gentle	penetrating	wind, wood	first daughter
☲	Li the Clinging	light–giving	fire	second daughter
☱	Tui the Joyous	joyful	lake	third daughter

Upper Trigram ► / Lower Trigram ▼	Ch'ien ☰	Chên ☳	K'an ☵	Kên ☶	K'un ☷	Sun ☴	Li ☲	Tui ☱
Ch'ien ☰	1	4	5	26	11	9	14	43
Chên ☳	25	51	3	27	24	42	21	17
K'an ☵	6	40	29	4	7	59	64	47
Kên ☶	33	62	39	52	15	53	56	31
K'un ☷	12	16	8	23	2	20	35	45
Sun ☴	44	32	48	18	46	57	50	28
Li ☲	13	55	63	22	36	37	30	49
Tui ☱	10	54	60	41	19	61	38	58

Key to the construction of the hexagrams

The world to which the hexagram's advice seems to apply, and the language in which it is given, make much of what is written in the I Ching strange at first glance. It is like trying to make sense of a fragment of poetry which has been translated from another language and another time. You will read of kings and princes, of lakes and mountains, of wanderers and sages, and wonder whether this can really apply to you. Sometimes. the very vagueness of the text allows it to have what seems to be a suitable meaning. It is possible to read into the words more than they actually hold. At other times, however, the advice can be very explicit.

Imagine that you are going to meet a man of slightly doubtful commercial reputation. You decide to ask of the I Ching whether he is to be trusted. The coins give Hexagram 13, 'Fellowship with Men'. Under the heading 'Judgement', are the following words:
'Fellowship with men in the open
Success
It furthers one to cross the great water
The perseverance of the superior man furthers'
The interpretation of this tells you, among other things, 'It is not the private interests of the individual that create lasting fellowship among men, but rather the goals of humanity. That is why it is said that fellowship with men in the open succeeds. If unity of this kind prevails, even difficult and dangerous tasks, such as crossing the great water, can be accomplished'.

Selection of lines

At this stage, another element enters the interpretation. Each line of the hexagram has a meaning, but you select only those lines for which you have thrown coins totalling either nine or six — in other words, all heads or all tails. These are the strong yang or yin lines and modify the general meaning of the oracle. When the coins total seven or eight, the lines have no individual meaning, but only help to build the hexagram. With a nine in the third line (reading, as one must, from the bottom up) this gives a new text:
'He hides weapons in the thicket
He climbs the high hill in front of it
For three years he does not rise up'
The interpretation of this (again in

Bottom left: In this engraving of a scene set in ancient China, yarrow sticks are being used. Above right: coins are a substitute for yarrow sticks in the casting of the hexagrams.

MALCOLM SCOULAR

part) is 'Obstacles standing in the way of fellowship with others are shown here. One has mental reservations for one's own part and seeks to take one's opponent by surprise. This very fact makes one mistrustful . . The result is that one departs further and further from true fellowship.'
All this seems to suggest that suspicions about the man you are to meet are unworthy and liable to do more harm than good. By not trusting him you will bring about the very situation which you fear. But the interpretation still needs one more phase.

Line reversal

When a strong yin or yang line, a line with the value nine or six, appears in a hexagram it has to be reversed, thus making a new hexagram which must in its turn be interpreted. Thus, the yang line, the unbroken line third from the bottom, was now changed to a broken yin line, and that gives Hexagram 25, Innocence (The Unexpected).
'Innocence. Supreme success.
Perseverance furthers.
If someone is not as he should be,
He has misfortune,
And it does not further him
To undertake anything.'
That is the Judgement, and its interpretation begins 'Man has received from heaven a nature innately good, to guide him in all his movements. By

devotion to this divine spirit within himself, he attains an unsullied innocence that leads him to do right with instinctive sureness and without any ulterior thought of reward and personal advantage.' So it would appear, finally, that as long as you are honest in your intentions and do not allow suspicion of this person to cloud your attitudes, everything will go very well.
The I Ching is a very seductive oracle. The very fact that it is not easy to grasp, that one has to work to make its messages clear, also makes it attractive.
However as the detailed example of interpretation shows, it can be practical, and it does seem to address itself to the problems raised. Of course, this is partly because the language of the I Ching is vague enough to apply to almost anything. Yet there are sixty-three other hexagrams which the coins might have chosen, many of which are much less well-adapted to answer a question dealing with suspicions about another person. Perhaps the ancient Chinese knew a thing or two about what makes coins fall in particular sequences, or why yarrow sticks should make patterns which are not really random at all. In any case, they have left us the I Ching, and whatever else its value may be, it certainly makes an unusual and absorbing game for agile-minded people who have an imaginative love of words.

The protection of amulets

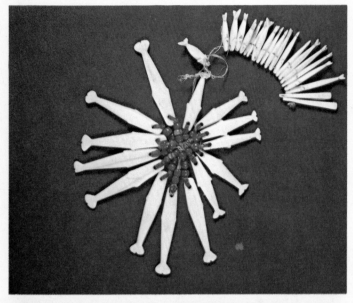

Amulets, talismans and lucky charms have been used since prehistoric times to ward off the evil effects of malignant forces, or as a sign of gratitude and devotion to benevolent ones. Lucky charms are still sold in great numbers, although charm bracelets now have a more or less decorative function. Most people have their own personal lucky charm — something they carry with them to examinations and important interviews, or always take on their journeys to help them arrive safely.

Nowadays, people are perhaps a little embarrassed about believing in charms. There is, however, still an element of 'just in case' about them, a feeling that they can help to protect one so it might be wiser not to discard them. In the past no such doubts existed; people were sure that they were vital insurance policies, to be discarded only at grave personal risk. Here are some amulets from different cultures and ages:

Above left: An Eskimo charm. The blue beads have mystical powers and the white whale — which the charm represents — was vital to the Eskimos' survival, so it, of course, often featured in their mythology.

Above right: A bead amulet worn by children of the Hadza tribe in Central Africa up until the middle of the twentieth century. This amulet was meant to protect the children from the evil and mystical effects associated with the calls of birds.

Below left: Egyptian funerary charms from the Pharaonic Middle Kingdom — 2133-1786 BC. These were supposed to help the deceased on the journey after death. Featured here: a scarab — the life symbol; a jet pillar of Osiris representing the backbone of the god and ensuring stability in the future life; and the eye of Horus: a symbol of health and happiness.

Below right: Northern Indian amulet of the early thirteenth century. This one, with the embossed figure, was worn by women who married widowers to protect them against the possibly malignant jealousy of the deceased wife.